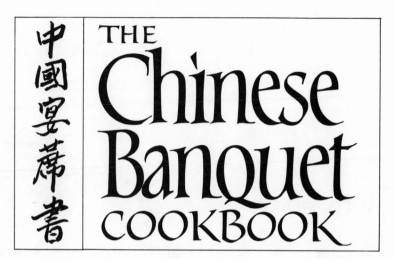

THE Chinese Banquet COOKBOOK

中國宴蓆書

Authentic
Feasts
from
China's
Regions

with

10 Complete
Banquets and
Over 100 Recipes

DRAWINGS
BY LAUREN JARRETT

CALLIGRAPHY BY SAN YAN WONG

THE Chinese Banquet COOKBOOK

中國宴蓆書

EILEEN YIN-FEI LO

CROWN PUBLISHERS, INC.
NEW YORK

Published by Crown Publishers, Inc., One Park Avenue, New York,
New York 10016, and simultaneously in Canada by General Publishing
Company Limited
Printed in the United States of America
Library of Congress Cataloging in Publication Data
Lo, Eileen Yin-Fei.
  The Chinese banquet cookbook.
  Includes index.
  1. Cookery, Chinese.   I. Title.
TX724.5.C5L5944   1985   641.5951   84-14315
ISBN 0-517-55521-2
Design by Lauren Dong
10 9 8 7 6 5 4 3 2 1
First Edition

For Stephen, Elena, Christopher, and Fred

Contents

Acknowledgments   ix

THE CHINESE BANQUET: An Introduction   1

THE BANQUET KITCHEN   11

The Foods   13
The Drink   34
The Tools   37
The Techniques   40

THE REGIONAL FEASTS   61

The First Course   63
Canton: Cooking of the South   75
Peking: Cooking of the North   93
Shanghai: Cooking of the East   113
Szechuan and Hunan: Cooking of the West   129
Hakka: Cooking of the Nomads   159
Hoi Sin: Food from the Water   179
Choy: Food from the Earth   195
Gung Hay Fat Choy: Cooking for a Happy New Year   211
Sweets: The Last Course   229

HO HO SIK: A Few Last Words   237

Index   239

Acknowledgments

When an idea for something special occurs to me, my excitement builds and I simply cannot wait to tell others about it. Happily for me there were those who not only listened, but shared my excitement and enthusiasm as well: my students and my friends; my "brother and sister," San and Rosanna Wong; Pamela Thomas, my editor, who more than helped an idea blossom into reality; Lauren Jarrett, whose art makes food live; and Joseph Spieler, my agent, who held my hand a lot. Thank you all.

There were times, as we tested and ate our way through the foods prepared for this book, that my family's collective patience and stomach capacities were truly tested. I recall one evening in particular, as I walked to the table bearing what must have been the eleventh version of one of the duck recipes, when all four of them quacked in mock rebellion. Thank you for only quacking. I love you, Stephen, Elena, Christopher, and Fred.

THE CHINESE BANQUET

An Introduction

To most Chinese, even in these post-revolution days, food is more than food. It is ritual, symbolism. What is eaten, when, how often, in what season, in what order, are often dictated by the writings of Confucius, by that Ch'ing dynasty gastronomic philosopher Yuan Mei, by the religions of Buddhism and Taoism, and by mythological beliefs.

Eat noodles on your sixtieth birthday, for then you will live longer. Cut the white portion of chicken neatly and precisely or it will not be fit to eat. Be certain there are bowls of tangerines and oranges in your house so that you, and those to whom you offer them, will be assured of sweetness in life. Before the New Year offer food to your ancestors so that they will not be "hungry ghosts." Be certain that a pregnant woman is given stalks of ripe grain. When a baby is born its first bath must contain fresh garlic and the leaves of the *wong pei,* a kumquatlike fruit. On the feast of the August Moon eat moon cakes filled with sweet lotus-seed paste so that in your next incarnation you will be beautiful.

In my house in Sun Tak, outside of Canton, when I was a little girl, we had a great, round lacquered box that was kept full of rice. So long as it was filled, my father told

1

me, we were a prosperous family. If it should become empty, we would be poor. In other parts of China it is customary to say that if you are working, "you have rice to chew on," while if you are out of work "your rice bowl is broken." Confucius wrote at one time that he thought more about the properties of food and its preparation than he did of preparations for war, and Lao Tzu suggested to China's emperors that they "rule a big country as you would fry small fish."

Few would doubt the Chinese preoccupation with food. There is even a God of the Kitchen whom we send to Heaven each year to say good things about us to the other gods. All year long the God of the Kitchen, *Jo Kwan*, hangs above the stove, a rather stern-looking fellow represented by an illustration on paper. Then, several days before the New Year, it is time for him to report, so we smear his lips with honey and burn his image. He rises up to Heaven and because of the honey he will say only sweet things about us.

Food, you see, is with us always. When someone is born we Chinese think of food; when a wedding is planned we think of food; holidays, religious and civil, are excuses for feasts; when someone dies, there is food.

It is a natural consequence of this historic reverence for food and of those beliefs that attribute life-giving, health-giving, peace-giving properties to different foods that a tradition of observing important events in life and in history and religion with particular foods, with feasts, with banquets should have arisen in China. Because China has an equally strong tradition for seeing to orderly arrangement, it is not surprising that a body of customs has arisen governing banquets.

The Ming dynasty, a 300-year reign from the middle of the fourteenth to the middle of the seventeenth century, established a Ministry of Rites to deal with the four levels of banquets mandated by the Imperial household, from Great to Minor, and gave almost equal status to both the chefs and those who secured foods for these feasts. There were different grades of non-Imperial banquets as well, those of sixteen dishes for rather important people, those of ten for the less important, those of eight for ordinary guests.

The Imperial Banqueting Court of the Manchus had six grades of banquets, not to mention a kitchen that prepared hundreds of dishes each day to present to the Dowager Empress so she could select the two or three that suited her fancy. The court ordered banquets by deciding upon the status of those guests invited.

Princes of China, from other provinces, usually were feted at the highest level, representatives from foreign missions, particularly Westerners, at the lowest level. Menus, which contained as many as forty dishes, would be scaled down accordingly. There were banquets for state visits, for royal births and weddings, for funerals, even for political exiles, when a banquet would be held at or near the gates of the city, with the person to be exiled, the dubious "guest of honor," seated so he could look in the direction to which he was headed.

Imperial banquets, particularly under the Ch'ing, China's last dynasty, from 1644 to 1911, often ran to many days, to more than thirty courses and hundreds of different dishes, all served in an order dictated by the court banquet department—fresh and preserved fruits first, fried foods next and those sweet with sugar and honey, preserved foods next, then meat, roasted, before going on to seafood. Wine, depending upon the importance of the occasion, was served continuously or at intervals in the feast.

Those are the banquets of history. There are some extravagant banquets today but nothing approaching those of more than a hundred dishes. About the closest, in terms of exotic food, is an Imperial banquet of thirty-seven dishes, served over the course of three days by Hong Kong's famous Sun Tung Lok Shark's Fin Restaurant.

One must diet before indulging in this three-day feast, which includes several different preparations of shark's fin, braised civet cat, duck flown in from Alaska, ovaries of snow frog topped with crab roe, braised bear's paw, roast suckling pig, ducks' tongues, and freshwater turtle.

There are special all-game banquets, given in Hong Kong's New Territories in a château called the Gay Villa where, if you arrange things several months in advance, you may enjoy a banquet of bear paw, wild boar, wild chicken, wild hare, snake, and deer, not to mention dessert, which is ginseng root. There are also the so-called *Bat Dai, Bat Siu* banquets that are considered sixteen-course banquets. The first eight courses are usually cold appetizers such as spiced cabbage, cold pork, chicken or beef, marinated shrimp, and mushrooms centered on a revolving tray or "lazy Susan" in the middle of the large banquet table. You sit around the table and eat them leisurely with your chopsticks, tasting one of the *bat siu*, the "eight small." Then come the *bat dai*, the "eight big," a parade of elaborately prepared hot dishes.

There is one of the most famous of Cantonese banquets, "Buddha Jumps Over the Wall," a banquet in a cauldron. This is made by adding ingredient after ingredient, as many as thirty, to a pot of broth. Some have suggested that it originated in the Ch'ing dynasty court, others that it was created in China's southern regions, where the food supply is varied and plentiful. I prefer to believe the latter.

If I am to believe an elderly chef from Canton, it should contain the following, at least: bamboo fiber, seeds from a thornbush called *gau gei ji*, the root called *bok chuk* (which by itself is supposed to cut fevers), turtle, chicken, duck, sea cucumbers, deer sinew, pig's tendons, shark's fin, dried abalone and scallops, fresh lamb, duck's gizzard, cured Hunan ham, and white fungus. Approximations of Buddha Jumps Over the Wall are served in this country and in Hong Kong. However, the Canton chef said that what is served in Hong Kong is not the true dish. That is not surprising, because in Hong Kong they say the version you can get in San Francisco is not true. In San

Francisco they say the New York version is but a pale imitation of the true dish.

They all agree, however, on the origin of its name. Buddha, who as everybody knows was a vegetarian, happened to be on the other side of a wall one day while this dish was cooking and it smelled so wonderful that, meat or not, he leaped over the wall to sample it. Thus its name.

In China today, most banquets are of ten courses. Most have cold preparations, or those served at room temperature, as first courses, and conclude with fresh fruit, usually oranges or apples, of which the Chinese are quite fond. The occasions for banquets vary. The one with which Westerners are most familiar is New Year's, the most important day of the year to the Chinese and the day for banquets, to which many Westerners are invited.

The New Year banquet, because it comes on the first day of the first month; because it symbolizes newness, rebirth, regeneration; because there are elements of religion in it, is perhaps the most important occasion of the year for all Chinese. It also happens to be everybody's birthday, no matter on which day you happened to be born, so it becomes a birthday party as well. The Chinese rarely celebrate birthdays; what they *do* celebrate is birth. One month after a baby is born, his parents give a banquet for him—or her. Birth announcements are not engraved cards but bowls of peanuts and chicken feet cooked in rice wine. On the day of the banquet, when the baby boy is a month old, red-dyed cooked chicken eggs are delivered to all of the unmarried sons of friends, relatives, and neighbors. If the baby is a girl, the gift is a red-dyed bun filled with red bean paste.

The gifts are given only to unmarried sons, not daughters. I recall being furious that my brother would get either an egg or a bun and I, a mere girl, would get nothing. I would put on a long face and my brother would give me his, but it still wasn't the same thing. I thought I should get an egg or a bun, too, even though my grandmother explained to me that the gifts were only for boys. She said that even stepsons didn't receive them. I still didn't feel any better, but I enjoyed the banquet, particularly the *sau toh*, the peach-shaped buns filled with sweet bean paste that *everybody* received.

Weddings were a bit more democratic when I was a girl, though not by much. There were two banquets on a wedding day, the feast given by the bridegroom's family, at which the groom and his new wife would be the guests of honor, and that given by the bride's family, to which only relatives and friends of that family were invited. It was explained to me that the bride had already been given to her husband and therefore was now part of his family. I must say I didn't care too much for that either, even though there was usually a third banquet a day later, to which both families and the wedding party came. It was at that banquet that the dragon and the phoenix were served—shrimp or lobster, "dragon," symbolizing the groom, and chicken, "phoenix," representing the bride.

I have said before that birthdays are rarely celebrated in China. That is true, but everybody celebrates the sixtieth birthday. It is usually a lovely banquet, the aim of which is to acknowledge that the celebrant is still around, to wish him or her continued long life, and to admire the long-life garment made just for the occasion. This is usually a robe of deep blue with silver and gold threads woven through it.

By wearing it the sixty-year-old is saying that he or she is now prepared to die happily, for the garment is never worn again while he or she lives. It is a burial garment. It is said that if there is no sixty-year-old garment, then the person will never rest in peace.

The banquet itself is a usual meal of ten courses, but it *has* to contain at least one noodle dish, for noodles too symbolize longevity. A sixtieth birthday party then is a sweet and a sad time. You are happy for your mother or father, for your aunt or uncle, or, in my case, for my grandmother, because she was still alive and I was able to kneel before her and offer her tea, sweet lotus seeds, and sugared wintermelon rind. But I was sad, as I ate the noodles, because I was reminded of her mortality.

I recalled that birthday banquet when, as a girl of nine, I attended my first funeral banquet, for my great-grand-aunt. I didn't wish to attend it, but my mother said it was my duty to go, so I went. I remember her house being filled with monks burning incense, and little fires of paper money and "gold" coins, and tiny houses and furniture, all sending things up to Heaven to make my great-grand-aunt more comfortable. And it was only the first banquet. There was another three weeks after she died, another at five weeks, yet another at seven weeks, still another one hundred days after her burial. Our family would eat a ten-course banquet at each occasion, but the monks would have a vegetarian banquet prepared for them.

As you can see, the banquet, the extended, elongated meal, is an important element in the lives of the Chinese. In Canton and in Shanghai there are even fund-raising banquets, quite a bit like those we are used to in the United States, except that these usually benefit an individual, usually a woman. It might be a woman recently widowed, or one whose husband had come upon hard times, "whose rice bowl was broken." Rather than simply give her money, which would be out and out charity and thus damaging to her pride, a banquet would be held. The woman would "collect" all the money and pay for the banquet. What was left belonged to her.

We banquet on such festivals as the August Moon, August 15, when we must eat moon cakes filled with sweet lotus-seed paste, salted duck egg yolks, sweet black beans, and fruits and nuts; and during the time of the Dragon Boat celebration, usually on May 5, when our banquet must contain a preparation of raw glutinous rice wrapped in bamboo leaves with beans, chestnuts, pork, and egg yolks. This is to commemorate the sacrifice of Chu Yuan, a poet and patriot of the Chou dynasty who, to protest governmental corruption, threw himself into the Mi Lo River and drowned. Local fishermen vainly tried to rescue him; failing that, they threw rice cakes into the river to aid his spirit. We banquet on New Year's Day, the day I always remember for having new clothes, getting red envelopes filled with "lucky money," and not combing my hair because I didn't wish to become a witch.

Families get together to banquet. Businessmen take over entire restaurants to hold banquets. People with the same surnames occasionally have banquets in honor of their name. Families get together around the banquet table.

This is not to suggest that a banquet is a daily occurrence for the Chinese. Banquets are for special occasions, for special times, and special observances. They are wonderful to anticipate, enjoyable to plan, satisfying to prepare, gratifying to serve.

The ideal banquet will seat ten people around a circular table and each person will be served ten courses in a carefully orchestrated manner. First dishes should engage the tongue and palate, arouse interest; then tastes should escalate, perhaps becoming sweet, then progressively more spicy, then hot. Then there should be a de-escalation so that the banquet will conclude with fish and perhaps a soothing bowl of rice. Care should be taken not to have tastes clash; a mild dish should not be followed by one hot and spicy. Rather, a mild course should be followed by one with perhaps more richness so that even as you eat that course you remember what has gone before. The idea is not to obliterate but to orchestrate.

Though this is the classic form, you need not prepare ten dishes for ten people. Why not do smaller feasts of four dishes, or five, for six people? One of the joys of Chinese cuisine is its adaptability.

I have not mentioned yields and servings in this book simply because it is meant to be a banquet book. Each recipe is meant to serve a small portion to each of ten people. Be guided by this. If you make six dishes for six people, four for four, for example, then, perforce, portions will be larger. Taken by itself each recipe yields four to six average portions. I have carefully tried to build a kind of flexibility into this book of banquets.

I have devoted even more care to the banquets themselves. Each recipe has its base in Chinese tradition. Most of the recipes are exactly as they have existed in China for years, centuries. Even a dessert like Fried Ice Cream is somewhat of a banquet staple in the more elegant restaurants of Canton, where the chefs are at their most creative. Other recipes, and I have noted these, are my creations, adaptations of traditional recipes, altered slightly for Western palates. In fact, the banquets themselves have been arranged so that they will, I trust, please both Western tastes and Chinese traditions. The menus for all the banquets in this book are arranged in the order in which I think they should be eaten. You may wish to change, to alter, to experiment.

So create a banquet for ten, for six, for three, even two, but be true to the tastes. *Ho Ho Sik,* or good eating, as we Cantonese say.

The Banquet Kitchen

The Foods

Chinese cooking is certainly a specialized cuisine. While many of the ingredients it requires are more readily available in neighborhood markets today, because of the increased interest in Chinese cooking, many are not. Most foods of Chinese origin, whether from the People's Republic of China, from Hong Kong or Taiwan, can be bought in Chinese and Asian markets. Most are available by mail order as well, particularly the prepared, preserved, and dried ingredients, and advertisements from the sellers can be found in the finer cookery magazines. Brands have also proliferated. I have refrained from specifying brands here except in such cases where I believe a particular brand of a food is far superior to its counterparts and thus essential to the recipes I offer.

Bamboo Shoots
These are the young beginnings of bamboo trees, spear-shaped. Rarely is the fresh variety available, and the occasional few that do reach markets are often discolored, dried out and, in general, unappetizing. Use those that have been cooked and canned in water. There are bamboo shoots and winter bamboo shoots, the latter considered more tender and of better quality. Cans will read "Winter Bamboo Shoots," or "Bamboo Shoots, Tips." The latter

13

are as good as those labeled "Winter" and are less expensive. Once the can is opened, shoots can be kept in water in a closed container. They will keep for 2 to 3 weeks if water is changed daily.

Bean Curd, Fresh

Called *dau fu* by the Chinese and *tofu* by the Japanese, bean curd comes in square cakes, 2½ to 3 inches on a side. Made from soybean liquid, or milk, the cakes have a custardlike consistency. I prefer the fresh, individual cakes rather than those that come several to a package, as they are sometimes sold. Bean curd has little taste of its own and its versatility lies in its ability to absorb the tastes of the foods it is combined with. It can be kept refrigerated in a container of water, tightly closed, with the water changed daily. So treated, it will keep for 2 to 3 weeks.

Bean Curd, Dried

When bean curd is being prepared, a film forms on top of the liquid. This is dried and cut into rectangular pieces about 1½ by 4 inches, and about ⅛ inch thick. Ideally it is sun-dried, but actually the drying in factories is under heat. The dried bean curd is brittle and should be handled carefully. Kept in a closed container, in a cool dry place, it will keep for at least a year.

Bean Curd Skins

Also a by-product of the cooking of soybean milk. Though it is the same film that forms in the cooking, this is thinner than dried bean curd, more flexible, and a bit moist. Usually it comes in round sheets, about 2 feet in diameter, but folded, 2 sheets to a plastic package, and is stored in the refrigerated sections of markets. It should be used as quickly as possible because it tends to become dry. It will keep no longer than a week and must be kept refrigerated. When using, take care to keep in a closed bag portions not being used, because exposure even for several minutes will dry the skins and make them brittle.

Bean Curd, "Wet"

Also called fermented or preserved bean curd, but the cans, jars, and crocks it comes in are labeled "Wet Bean Curd." It consists of small cakes of bean curd, cured with salt, wine, and either chilies or "red rice." Red rice is just that, a rice reddish in color, used basically as a vegetable dye. For use with this book the "Wet Bean Curd" referred to is that with red rice added. It is more fragrant than the other kind and adds fine flavor to barbecued pork.

Bean Thread Noodles

Often called simply bean threads, or vermicelli bean threads, or cellophane noodles. They are made when mung beans are moistened, mashed, and strained, and formed from the substance that is left. They come in ½-pound packages or in 2-ounce packs, eight to a 1-pound package.

Black Beans, Fermented

These wonderfully fragrant beans are preserved in salt. They come in plastic packages and cans. I prefer those in packages, lightly flavored with orange peel and ginger. Before they are used, the salt should be rinsed off. They can be kept for as long as a year, without refrigeration, so long as they are in a tightly sealed container.

Brown Bean Sauce

Also called yellow or ground bean sauce. It is made from fermented soybeans and wheat flour with sugar and soy sauce added.

Bok Choy

Perhaps the most famous vegetable in Canton, where it is called the white vegetable. The white-stalked, green-leafed vegetable, so versatile in Chinese cookery, is sweet and juicy. It is sold by weight. It is often called "Chinese Cabbage," but that is a misnomer because it bears no resemblance to cabbage. It will keep for about a week in the vegetable drawer of a refrigerater, but it tends to lose its sweetness quickly, so I recommend using it when it is fresh.

Bok Choy, Shanghai

This is a very special vegetable. Although it is more widely available than before, it was at one time rare in Canton, virtually unobtainable in Hong Kong. It is a Shanghai original that looks a bit like a fennel plant around the bulbous stalk section, but with leaves resembling bok choy. The whiter the stalks, the heavier the head, the better. It should be used as quickly as possible, no later than 3 days after its purchase, because it loses its taste and its leaves become yellow.

Cabbage, Shanghai

The Chinese call this *hsueh loi hung,* or "Red Inside Snow," even though the leafy vegetable is all green. It resembles collard greens. The Chinese rarely eat it fresh. More often, it is preserved in salt and cut up for use in soups, or with noodles, meats, and fish. It is available in cans labeled "Shanghai Cabbage." Fresh cabbage, boiled and salted, will keep in a closed jar, refrigerated, for a year.

Catsup

The catsup from China comes in bottles, like its Western counterpart. It is made from tomatoes, vinegar, and spices. The difference between it and Western catsup, with which we are familiar, is its use. In China catsup is used more as a food-coloring agent than as a flavoring. It is difficult to obtain, however, so the use of usual catsup will suffice.

Celery Cabbage

Often called "Tientsin Cabbage" or "Tientsin Bok Choy," it comes in two varieties, either with a long stalk, or a rounder sort, which is much leafier. It is the latter variety that is most often referred to along with its city of origin,

Tientsin. It is also the sweeter of the two and I prefer it. It is at its best in the spring. It may be kept, refrigerated, in a plastic bag for about a week, but, like bok choy, it tends to lose its sweetness, so I suggest using it early.

Choi Sum
A green leafy vegetable with thin, tender stalks. It has large leaves on the outside, smaller ones inside. The stalks are light green, crisp, and sweet. Choi sum, like other fresh leafy vegetables, tends to lose its sweetness and so should be eaten as soon as possible.

Chili Paste
A paste of chili peppers with garlic.

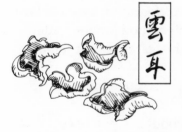

Cloud Ears
Also called Tree Ears. They are fungi that when dried look a bit like round, dried-up chips of brown and brownish-black. When they are soaked in hot water they soften and resemble flower petals. They may be kept in a closed jar, in a cool dry place, indefinitely.

Coriander
Similar in appearance to parsley, it is also called cilantro and "Chinese Parsley." It has a strong aroma and taste; when used either as a flavoring agent or as a garnish, it is distinctive. Often it is suggested that Italian parsley be used as a substitute. To me there is no substitute for coriander. It should be used fresh so that its bouquet will be appreciated, but it can be kept refrigerated for a week to 10 days.

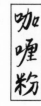

Curry Powder
There are many brands of curry powder on the market. I prefer the stronger, more pungent brands from India.

Eggplant, Chinese
Bright purple eggplant, shaped somewhat like a cucumber and about the same size. Its taste is like that of the eggplant most of us are used to, but its skin is quite tender and need not be peeled before cooking.

Eight-Star Anise
Often called Star Anise, this is a tiny 8-pointed hard star. Its flavor is more pronounced than that of aniseed. It should be kept in a tightly sealed jar in a cool dry place. It will keep for a year, but will gradually lose its fragrance.

Five-Spice Powder
A powder that imparts a distinctive taste of anise to food. It can be made of a combination of spices including star anise, fennel seeds, cinnamon, cloves, gingerroot, licorice, nutmeg, and Szechuan peppercorns. Obviously there are more than five spices listed, but different makers use different combinations. Anise and cinnamon predominate. It should be stored similarly to Eight-Star Anise. It tends to lose its fragrance after 6 months.

Gingerroot
One substance you cannot do without in Chinese cookery. When selecting gingerroots, look for those with smooth outer skins, because like many of us, ginger begins to wrinkle and roughen with age. It flavors, it is used to diffuse strong fish and shellfish odors, and the Chinese say that it greatly reduces stomach acidity. It is used rather sparingly. It should be sliced and peeled before use. When placed in a heavy brown paper bag and refrigerated, it will keep for 4 to 6 weeks. I do not recommend trying to preserve it in wine, or freezing it, because it loses strength. Nor do I recommend ground ginger or bottled ginger juice as cooking substitutes, because for ginger there is no substitute.

Ginger Juice
This is available in small bottles, but you can make a better

quality yourself simply by cutting fresh ginger into small pieces and pressing them in a garlic press. Do not store it. Make it as needed.

Ginger Pickle
Young ginger pickled with salt, sugar, and white vinegar (see page 72), made from young ginger, pinkish white and smooth, without the toughened gnarled skin of older ginger; it is quite crisp. Quite often it is mistakenly called spring ginger; it grows not in the spring but twice each year, late in the summer and in January and February.

Gingko Nuts
These are hard-shelled nuts shaped like tiny footballs, which are the seeds in the fruit of the gingko tree, a common shade tree in China. The fruit is not edible, but the nuts, when cooked, are. Pale green when raw, they become translucent when cooked. They are available fresh or canned. When fresh, they require cooking; the canned sort are already cooked. Raw nuts will keep, refrigerated in a plastic bag, for 4 to 6 weeks. Cooked, they will keep for only 4 to 5 days. Canned nuts, when opened, should be used within a week. Both should be refrigerated.

Glutinous Rice
It is often called "Sweet Rice" and is shorter grained than other rice and when cooked becomes somewhat sticky. Its kernels stick together in a mass instead of separating the way long-grain rice does.

Glutinous Rice Powder
Flour ground from glutinous rice. It is so fine a flour that we call it powder.

Green Tea
The Long Jin green tea from the region around Hangzhou. It is wonderful to drink. When used as an ingredient to smoke foods, it imparts a delicate aroma.

Hoisin Sauce

A thick, chocolate-brown sauce made from soybeans, garlic, sugar, and chilies. Some brands add a little vinegar, others thicken the sauce with flour. It is best known as a complement to Peking Duck. Hoisin comes in large cans or jars. If in a can, it should be transferred to jars and kept refrigerated. It will keep for many months.

Horse Beans

Broad beans, somewhat like lima beans, that come four or five to the pod. The Chinese like young beans fried, boiled, or baked. They are also available dried, salted, and preserved.

Hot Oil

This can be bought, but you'll be more satisfied with your own. Here's how to make it: Add ½ cup of dried hot red pepper flakes to ¾ cup sesame oil and ¾ cup peanut oil. Put all in a large jar, mix, close the jar tightly, and put in a cool dry place for 4 weeks. It will then be ready for use. It will keep indefinitely.

Hunan Pepper

The soaked pepper flakes at the bottom of the hot oil.

Lop Cheung

Chinese sausages, traditionally made of pork, pork liver, and duck liver. Very little duck-liver sausage is available in the United States, however. Most common are pork sausages, usually in pairs, threaded through with pork fat, held together by string. They are cured but not cooked, and thus must be cooked before eating. They can be kept refrigerated for about a month, and when frozen, from 3 to 4 months. A somewhat leaner pork sausage from Canadian processors is also available in some markets, but in my view it lacks the distinctive flavor of those made in the United States.

Lotus leaves

Bamboo leaves

Lotus Leaves or Bamboo Leaves

Dried leaves used as wrappings for various steamed preparations. Lotus leaves impart a distinctive, somewhat sweet taste and aroma to the food they are wrapped around, and they are preferred to bamboo leaves. However, lotus leaves are usually sold commercially only to restaurants in 50-pound boxes. Bamboo leaves can be easily bought in smaller quantities and are admirable substitutes, but they have a very different taste and smell. Kept in a plastic bag in a dry place the dried leaves will keep for 6 months to a year.

NOTE: If you are able to get fresh lotus leaves, then by all means use them fresh, or sun-dry them yourself for future use.

Lotus Root

The gourd-shaped root of the lotus. Often four or five grow together, connected like a string of sausages, each about 2 ½ inches in diameter, 4 to 6 inches long. When the root is cut through, there is a pattern of holes, not unlike Swiss cheese. The texture is light and crunchy. Lotus root should be kept refrigerated in a brown paper bag and used within a few days of purchase, since it tends to lose flavor and texture.

Lotus Seeds

The olive-shaped seeds from the lotus pod. They are regarded as a delicacy and priced accordingly, by weight. They can be kept for as long as a month in a tightly sealed jar at room temperature. I do not recommend keeping them that long, however, because their texture roughens and their flavor weakens.

Mushrooms, Black Dried

These are very much a staple of Chinese cooking, not only for their distinctive flavor, but for their versatility. They come in boxes or in cellophane packs. They are black, dark

gray, brownish-black, or speckled, and range in size from those with caps about the size of a nickel to those with diameters of 3 inches. Those in boxes are choice in size and color and are, of course, more expensive. They must always be soaked in hot water for at least 30 minutes before use, the stems removed and discarded, and they should be thoroughly cleaned on the underside of the cap, then squeezed dry. Dry, they will keep indefinitely in a tightly closed container, in a cool dry place. If you live in an especially damp or humid climate they should be stored in the freezer.

Mustard Greens

Leafy, cabbagelike vegetable called *kai choi* by the Chinese, or Leaf-Mustard Cabbage. It is used fresh in soups or stir-fried with meats, but it is more commonly used in its preserved forms. Water-blanched and cured with salt and vinegar, it is used in stir-fries or soups. It comes loose by weight, or in cans. The cans will read "Sour Mustard Pickle," or "Sour Mustard Greens," or simply "Mustard Greens." If bought loose, place them in a tight plastic container and keep, refrigerated, for not more than 2 weeks. Once cans are opened, greens should be stored in the same manner and have the same storage life. The taste is strong and distinctive.

Mustard Greens, Preserved

Although this vegetable is from the same family as the preceding, it is a different species called *chuk gai*, or "Bamboo Mustard"; it grows in the southern part of China. It can be eaten fresh, but is also more commonly used in a preserved form. In this case the vegetable is quickly boiled, then preserved only in salt, dried, and sold in packages only. It is not canned. Once cured, it is called *mui choi* by the Chinese. Because no vinegar is used in the curing, it is less sour than Mustard Greens. The preserved greens are used in steaming processes.

Mustard Pickle

Also called Szechuan Mustard Pickle, it is made with Chinese radishes cooked with chili powder and salt. It can be added to soups and stir-fried with vegetables. It is never used fresh, only in its preserved form. It can be bought loose by weight, but more often can be found in cans, labeled "Szechuan Preserved Vegetables" or "Szechuan Mustard Pickle."

NOTE: As you can see from the preceding ingredients, there can be instances of loose labeling, so be careful when you buy, so you obtain the correct vegetable.

Ng Ga Pay or Ngapei

A strong, 96-proof distilled spirit, of either rice or wheat. It is made in the People's Republic of China, in Hong Kong and Taiwan, and comes both in bottles and in distinctive brown ceramic jugs.

Oyster Sauce

A thick sauce of oyster extract and salt. It imparts a rich taste to many dishes. There are many brands, but I prefer bottles labeled "Hop Sing Lung," manufactured and bottled in Hong Kong.

Red Bean Paste

A thick paste made from cooked mashed red beans, sweetened with sugar. It is used as a pastry or sweet dessert filling. It comes in cans. Once opened and refrigerated in a closed container, it will keep for 4 to 6 weeks.

Rice Noodles

Also called Rice Sticks and Rice Vermicelli. Very fine noodles made from rice that come in 1-pound packages. They are made in, and imported from, Thailand, Hong Kong, and the People's Republic. I prefer the superior quality of a Chinese brand called Double Swallow. The noodles, packed in plastic bags and kept in a cool dry place, will keep for a year.

Rock Candy

Or rock sugar; a compound of white sugar, raw brown sugar, and honey. It comes in 1-pound packs and looks like a collection of light amber rocks.

Sand Ginger

A dark brown root, smaller and more gnarled than regular gingerroot. The roots are available sliced and dried or as powder, both packed in plastic envelopes. The envelope for the dried pieces is labeled "Kapurkachi." The label for the powder will read "Kaempferia Galanga." It is wonderfully aromatic. Both the dried root and the powder should be kept in tightly sealed containers in a cool dry place; they will keep for a year. However, as the root ages it tends to lose some of its fragrance.

Sausages, Chinese

See Lop Cheung.

Scallion Oil

This is an ingredient that cannot be bought in markets. It was created by an elderly chef who told me what its ingredients were. I created the recipe. It is a delicious ingredient when added to recipes. Here is how you make it:

Ingredients
1 cup of the stringy whiskers end of scallions, washed and dried thoroughly
1 cup green portions of scallions, cut into 3 sections, washed and dried thoroughly
3 cups peanut oil

Directions
Heat a wok over medium heat. Add peanut oil, then add all scallions. When scallions brown, the oil is done. With a strainer, remove and discard scallions. Strain the oil through a fine strainer into a mixing bowl and allow to cool to room temperature. Pour scallion oil into a glass jar and refrigerate until needed. Makes 3 cups. It will keep for about 2 months. The recipe may be cut into halves or thirds.

Sesame Oil

An aromatic oil with a strong, almost nutlike smell that is used both as a cooking oil and as an additive or dressing. It is made from sesame seeds. Adding a bit to an already prepared dish imparts fine flavor, particularly in the case of some soups. It is thick and brown in versions from China and Japan, thinner and lighter from the Middle East. I recommend the former. Store in a tightly capped bottle at room temperature; it will keep for at least 4 months.

Shanghai Bok Choy

See Bok Choy, Shanghai.

Shanghai Cabbage

See Cabbage, Shanghai.

Shanghai Wine Pills

See Wine Pills, Shanghai.

Shao-Hsing Wine

A sherrylike rice wine made and bottled in the People's Republic of China and in Taiwan.

Shark's Fin

The fin of a shark. Usually sold in dried form in packages, it must be cooked repeatedly until it comes to the noodle-like consistency favored for soups. A great, and expensive, delicacy. It also comes frozen, ready to use. I prefer preparing it myself, but it *is* time-consuming. The packages of dried fins, stored at room temperature in a cool dry place, will keep for many months.

Shrimp Chips

Thin, hard chips that come in bright, translucent colors. They are about the size of a quarter and look a bit like hard candy. Made of shrimp essence, they puff up, much like a thick potato chip, when deep-fried. They can be eaten like chips or used to garnish other dishes. They come in cardboard boxes. Once opened, they should be kept in a tightly closed container; they will keep indefinitely.

Soy Sauces

Either light or dark. The light soys are usually taken from the top of the batches being prepared, the darker soys from the bottom. Both are made from soybeans, flour, salt, and water. There are many brands, but I believe the best quality to buy is a Hong Kong brand called Yuet Heung Yuen.

The light soy sauce from this manufacturer is labeled "Pure Soy Bean Sauce"; the dark soy (it is often called Double-Dark) is marked "'C' Soy Sauce." Dark soys are best with meats, for roasting, for sauces, for rich dark coloring. Light soys are best for shrimp, chicken, and pork. There is even a soy with mushroom flavoring, and bottles of this dark soy are so labeled. The Chinese believe rightly that they give a sweetness of taste to other foods. I often combine the various soys for different tastes and colorings. Experiment yourself.

Some soy sauces come in cans, though most come bottled. If in a can, transfer it to a bottle. It can be kept in a tightly capped bottle at room temperature indefinitely.

Straw Mushrooms

A species of mushroom common in southern China, rare here. Usually markets carry them dry or in cans, cooked. Dried mushrooms should be stored like other dried mushrooms and reconstituted before use. Those in cans should be used as quickly as possible after the can is opened. An odd-looking species, the mushrooms have tiny pointed caps. In fact they look like tiny, fat evergreens, tan to light brown in color.

Sweet Wine Rice

See page 230.

Szechuan Peppercorns

Quite different from the usual peppercorn. This peppercorn is reddish in color, not solid, but open. The Chinese often call it "Flower Peppercorn" because of its shape. It is not peppery, but rather mild. You may buy these fresh and roast them yourself, or buy them roasted. Store in a tightly capped jar as you would ordinary peppercorns. To make *Szechuan Ground Pepper*, grind the corns in a mortar with a pestle, or smash with the broad side of a cleaver blade, then strain through a sieve. Store in a tightly closed jar. Szechuan ground pepper cannot be bought. You must make it yourself.

Szechuan Mustard Pickle
See Mustard Pickle.

Szechuan Preserved Vegetables
See Mustard Pickle.

Tapioca Flour
Tapioca starch, as it is often called, is made from the starch of the cassava root, and much of it comes packaged from Thailand. It is used as a basic ingredient in some dim sum doughs, as a thickener for sauces, or as a coating. Store as you would any flour.

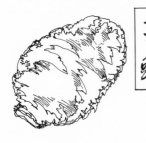

Taro Root
This is the starchy root of the tropical taro plant, often called *poi*, as it is in Hawaii. It is somewhat like a potato but more fibrous, and is tinged with purplish threads throughout its interior. As it steams it emits a chestnutlike aroma. It must be eaten cooked, usually steamed and mashed. It may be stored briefly in the vegetable drawer of a refrigerator.

Tientsin Cabbage
See Celery Cabbage.

Tiger Lily Buds
Elongated, reddish-brown lily buds that have been dried. They are also known as "Golden Needles." The best sort are those that have softness to them and are not dry and brittle. Sold in packages, they will keep indefinitely in a tightly covered jar stored in a cool dry place.

Water Chestnuts

These are not actually nuts; they are bulbs, deep purplish-brown in color, that grow in muddy water. To peel freshwater chestnuts is time-consuming, but once accomplished the meat of the water chestnut is sweet, juicy, crunchy, and utterly delicious. Canned water chestnuts are a barely adequate, though serviceable, substitute, and to search for fresh ones is most rewarding. Quite versatile, they can be eaten raw or lightly stir-fried with meats, poultry, and other vegetables. They are even ground into a flour to be used as the basis for pastry.

They should be eaten while very fresh to enjoy them the most. As they age they become less firm, more starchy, less sweet. If you keep the skins on, with mud remnants on them, and refrigerate them in a brown paper bag, they will keep for 4 to 5 weeks. Peeled and placed in a container with cold water and refrigerated, they will keep for 4 to 5 days, provided the water is changed daily. Canned water chestnuts can be stored similarly.

Wheat Starch

The remains of wheat flour when the wheat's protein is removed to make gluten. This starch is the basis for dim sum wrappings and has other uses as well. These powders will keep for at least a year if stored in a tightly sealed container and kept in a cool dry place.

Wine Pills, Shanghai

Very hard round white balls, about the size of large marbles; basically balls of yeast which function as fermenting agents. They are packed two to a small plastic bag. They are dried and hard and will last for months.

Wine, Chablis

In China a white wine called *Bok Jau* is used in various seafood preparations. For years this was unavailable. These days Bok Jau can be bought in Chinatowns and in many Asian food markets, where it is often labeled "Chinese Cooking Wine." I use Chablis in its place, because I find the two wines quite alike for cooking purposes.

Wintermelon
This looks a bit like watermelon and grows to the same oblong-round shape. Its skin is dark green and occasionally mottled, while the interior is greenish white with white seeds. Wintermelon has the characteristic of absorbing the flavors of whatever it is cooked with. When it is cooked, usually in soup or steamed, the melon becomes beautifully translucent. Often the whole melon is used as a tureen, with other ingredients steamed inside it after it has been hollowed out a bit and seeded. It should be used almost immediately, for it tends to dry quickly, particularly when pieces are cut from a larger melon. It is usually sold by weight.

Yellow Chives
A variety of chive that is bright yellow in color, rather than the customary green. They are grown in the dark and have a decided, strong onion taste. They are often chopped and put into soup or stir-fried. They are most tender but should be eaten immediately, for their storage life, even refrigerated, is no more than 2 days.

Shopping Guide to Fowl

Chicken
Always try to buy fresh-killed chickens if available. (You may wish to use the neck and inner parts of a fresh-killed chicken for soups or stock.) If possible buy those which have been hand-plucked. Chickens usually are dipped into boiling water in order to facilitate removal of feathers by machine. This is not the case with hand-plucked chickens. The taste is infinitely better.

If you are buying chicken that is not freshly killed, first look for the date on the package in which it is wrapped. If the date has expired, do not buy it. Check to see if the chicken has been frozen. Usually frozen chickens have been allowed to defrost in meat cases. Often they will be hard to the touch and there will be traces of crystallization. If a chicken has been in a display case too long, its packaging will contain too much reddish, blood-colored liquid. If you buy chicken cutlets, ask your butcher to remove them from a whole chicken breast, rather than buy them packaged.

Duck

Ducks should be fresh-killed as well. (The neck and inner portions, like those of chickens, can be used for soups and stocks.) Look for dates. All of the shopping criteria for chickens apply to ducks as well.

For Peking Duck, fresh-killed duck is highly preferred. In China a species called Pekin Duck, used for this preparation, are raised specially. They are confined to tiny spaces, are not permitted to run free, and are force-fed so that they will grow fatter than normal, their breasts will be larger than usual, and their meat more tender. This method of raising ducks is considered cruel in the West. Thus I suggest fresh-killed ducks, preferably the Long Island variety, which are quite good and weighty. A source for fresh-killed ducks would be a kosher poultry shop. For Peking Duck the head, wings, and feet should be left on for best cooking results.

If fresh-killed ducks are not available, frozen ducks may be used. Again, look for dates and signs that will indicate relative freshness (or lack of it) before making your purchase. Frozen ducks can be used in all recipes; however, a duck frozen and with its head removed will be difficult to use for Peking Duck because in that preparation the skin must be separated from the flesh, usually by air pressure; this is impossible with a headless duck. What you will have to do, if you use a headless duck for Peking Duck, is to separate the skin from the flesh by hand.

Shopping Guide to Meat

Pork
When you have access to fine-quality fresh pork as we have, for example, in New Jersey, then you can buy with confidence. The use of a butcher is recommended, however. When pork is mentioned in these recipes I suggest use of double-cut pork chops, fresh pork butt, or fresh ham, all of which can be supplied by a butcher. In a supermarket those cuts are available packaged. A sign that packaged pork has been lying about in a meat case too long is an excessive amount of liquid in the package and a dull color to the meat. Fresh pork will be quite pink.

Beef
Buy fresh beef, preferably from a butcher, and age it yourself before using. Allow beef to rest in the meat-keeping compartment of a refrigerator for several days until liquid drains off and meat turns from bright red to darker brownish-red.

Specific recommended cuts include:

London Broil. Look for the "oyster cut," which is a bit smaller than regular London Broil. It is shaped like an elongated oval, somewhat pinched in the center, like two oysters side by side. A kosher butcher will know this cut readily; others may not, so be specific.

Flank Steak. Choose thick flank steak because it is easier to slice and to shred for such dishes as orange beef and curried beef.

Shopping Guide to Fish and Seafood

Striped Bass
This is an exceptionally tasty fish with firm flesh. It also has fewer bones than fish such as carp and bluefish. It is not always available.

Sea Bass
I believe this to be not quite so tasty as striped bass, but it still has a fine flavor and a firm texture. It is also cheaper than striped bass and easier to obtain.

Red Snapper
Quite like Sea Bass in most respects, Red Snapper can be substituted wherever Sea Bass is called for.

Flounder
Flat fish, easily obtainable, can be used in steamed and panfried recipes if either bass is unavailable. However, flounder has a different taste, which is most pleasant, and softer flesh, so takes less time to cook.

Carp
This is a fish with many bones but with a fine, sweet taste. When it is small, from 2 to 3 pounds, it is exceptionally bony and is not recommended. Buy by the piece. Have your fish dealer cut a thick slice from the center of the body of a carp that weighs at least 8 to 10 pounds. The bones will be bigger and easier to remove. Carp is oily but extremely tasty; it is the fish I remember most from my childhood.

In general, when you are buying fish, any fish, buy freshness. Look for eyes that are clear, not cloudy; gills that are red. If fish has been frozen, the eyes will seem to have sunk into the head.

Shrimp
Fresh fish is virtually unobtainable in most parts of the United States. Notable exceptions are areas around the Gulf of Mexico, occasionally in Maine. But you will probably buy frozen shrimp that have been defrosted. Look for those of a gray color. Pink color indicates the shrimp have been dropped into boiling water briefly, then frozen. These are not recommended.

Lobster
Should be fresh, and freshly killed in front of you before buying. Or you may kill it yourself. Frozen lobster has a dull, uninteresting taste, while fresh lobster is sweet, juicy, and has a wonderful, crunchy texture. The size I recommend for tenderness is 1½ to 2 pounds.

Scallops
These days it is difficult to tell fresh sea scallops from *faux* scallops, which have been stamped by machine out of shark meat or from the meaty wings of the manta ray. If the market price seems inordinately expensive, they are usually genuine scallops. Unfortunately, it is easy to tell real scallops from fakes only after cooking. Those not real will often have offensive, excessively fishy aromas. The best advice I can give is to buy your scallops from a reliable fishmonger.

The Drink

Traditionally wine was drunk with Imperial banquets, usually a strong rice wine, but in the course of time what is drunk with banquets has changed. These days it is perfectly proper to drink wine, beer, whiskey, brandy or Cognac, or tea, either as a choice for the entire meal, or in combination.

Attempts have been made to match wines with Chinese food, but they rarely succeed, simply because the tastes of Chinese food, particularly in a varied ten-course banquet, are so different, elusive, subtle. I suggest, if you wish to drink wine, that you choose a fine, dry Chablis or an equally fine Alsatian Gewürztraminer. Make certain it is nicely chilled and stay with it through the entire feast.

Wines *can* of course be matched to Chinese foods, but the number of tastings required to make perfect matches is perhaps beyond the pocketbooks and patience of most people. However, it *is* possible. Here is an example:

Not long ago, the Brotherhood of the Knights of the Vine, a society with a love of and devotion to American wines, asked me to devise a banquet to be eaten with American wines only. We tasted more than 30 wines with different foods before settling upon the final selections. The banquet with its wines turned out to be fine combinations indeed. Reprinted below is the menu with its matching wines.

HONEY WALNUTS	*Robert Hunter Sonoma Valley*
BATTER-FRIED	*Brut de Noirs*
OYSTERS	
A DIM SUM	*Landmark White Table, Sonoma*
SELECTION	
SAUTÉED CHICKEN	*Stratford California Chardonnay*
BREASTS WITH	
WATERCRESS	
POACHED SEA BASS	*Mount Eden Vineyards*
(White Water Fish)	*Santa Cruz Mountain*
	Chardonnay
SPICY LOBSTER	*Simi Mendocino Gewürztraminer*
SHARK'S FIN SOUP	
WITH SHREDDED	
CHICKEN AND	
SNOW PEAS	
ORANGE BEEF	*Wickham Vineyards*
	New York State Johannisberg
	Riesling
FRIED RICE	*Vichon Napa Cabernet*
YANGZHOU	*Fay Vineyard*
STYLE	
PEKING DUCK	*Sanford Vineyards Santa Maria*
	Valley
	Pinot Noir
COLD FRESH FRUITS	*Freemark Abbey Edelwein Gold*
	Sweet Johannisberg Riesling

For purposes of going from white to red wines, Peking Duck was placed at the end of the banquet; aside from that, the orchestration I insist upon was there, as tastes went from steamed to spicy. Each dish in the banquet, except for the sautéed chicken breasts and the dim sum (the recipes for which are in my previous book, *The Dim Sum Book: Classic Recipes from the Chinese Teahouse*), is to be found in this book. So you might try duplicating that banquet for yourself.

Cold beer is equally at home at a banquet. A recent innovation, particularly during banquets within the People's Republic of China, has been to offer diners a choice. It is not unusual to sit at a table and find, lined up at your right, a glass of that fiery wheat-and-millet-based liquor called Mou-Tai, another of sweet plum wine, another of beer, still another of orange soda, and finally a cup of tea. It is the Chinese way of saying, do not be embarrassed, drink what you wish.

Still another recent custom is to drink either Shao-Hsing wine or a Cognac or brandy. To the Chinese drinking Cognac or brandy at a banquet means *drinking*. It is not at all unusual to have several bottles of it finished in the course of a banquet.

I prefer tea. Tea cleanses the palate, it soothes the stomach, and it is delicious. I would recommend several teas for drinking at a banquet. *Jasmine* tea is wonderfully fragrant and has a clean, precise taste that goes quite well with highly flavored or spicy foods. *Long Jin* or *Lung Ching* or *Dragon Well*, depending upon the package you buy, is that justly famous green tea from Hangzhou. I use it to tea-smoke duck, but drinking it helps to stimulate the appetite. *Tiht Koon Yum* is an oolong tea named for Teh Kuan Yin, the Chinese mythological Goddess of Mercy. It is dark, metallic green; it is said that it both cuts the effects of grease and oil and stimulates the appetite. That is also said about *Soi Sin*, another oolong that is slightly bitter.

You may wish to drink different teas with different parts of your banquet. This is not at all unusual; we Chinese do it all the time. I recommend that with your dessert, either fruit or sweet, you drink *Lichee Black* tea, which has a lovely aroma not unlike that of those sweet fruits.

The Tools

It is often thought that since the varieties of Chinese cookery seem enormous, there must be an equally enormous number of tools to prepare them. This is really not so. In fact, you can create a Chinese kitchen with a minimum of equipment.

You need that most basic of Chinese cook pots, the wok, and a few other Chinese tools. The remainder, as you will see, will most likely be in your kitchen drawers and cabinets already.

Wok

There are many woks available these days, unfortunately most of them inadequate. The best you can buy is one of carbon steel, with a diameter of about 14 inches. It is the all-purpose Chinese cooking utensil that can be used for stir-frying and deep-frying; with the addition of bamboo steamers, it is a foolproof steamer as well. The seasoning and care of the wok is discussed in the section on cooking techniques, page 41.

Wok Ring

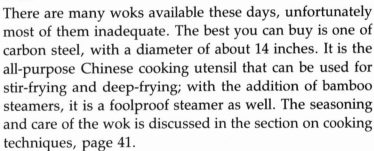

A steel, hollow base that fits over a single stove burner. The wok base nestles into it, thus assuring that the wok will sit firmly, and also that the round base of the wok will reach into the flames of the burner.

Bamboo Steamer

These are circles of bamboo with woven bamboo reed bases and covers. They come in various sizes, but those 12 to 13 inches in diameter are preferred. Foods sit on the woven bamboo and steam passes up through the spaces. They can be stacked two or three high so that different foods can be steamed simultaneously. Steamers are also made of aluminum, and of wood with bamboo mesh bases; there are small steamers, usually of bamboo or stainless steel, that are often used for individual dim sum brunch servings. For use with the recipes in this book two bamboo steamers and a cover should be sufficient.

Chinese Spatula

This is a shovel-shaped tool available in either carbon or stainless steel, and in different sizes. I prefer a medium-size carbon-steel spatula.

Chinese Cleaver

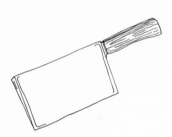

This is still another all-purpose tool. It cuts, dices; its flat blade and its handle can mash. Usually of carbon steel with wood handle, it is also available in stainless steel, either with a similar wood handle or as a one-piece tool with blade and handle of one piece of steel.

The carbon steel is preferred because of its keener edge and because it is capable of such heavy-duty jobs as cleaving through bone. The preferred size is one with a blade 8 inches long and between 3½ and 3¾ inches wide.

You may prefer to have a second cleaver, of stainless steel, with a blade 8 inches long by 3¼ inches wide, of much lighter weight. The cleaver is perfect for slicing. Chinese cooks call it their "Chef's Knife."

Bamboo Chopsticks

These are useful tools in addition to being what the Chinese eat with. They are fine stirrers, mixers, and serving pieces. They are available usually in packages of 10, for under $1.00. Avoid plastic chopsticks. They cannot be used for cooking and they are more difficult to manipulate than those of bamboo.

Chinese Strainer
A circular steel-mesh strainer attached to a long split-bamboo handle. Strainers come in many sizes, from as small as the average palm to as large as 14 inches in diameter. For all-purpose use I prefer one 10 inches in diameter.

In addition to the specialized utensils listed above, I suggest the following to complete your Chinese kitchen:

oval Dutch oven
large roasting pans
frying pan, cast iron, 10 inches in diameter
round cake pan
selection of heatproof dishes
china dishes
strainer, a fine, all-purpose household strainer
rolling pin, heavy hardwood
cutting board, wood preferred
wood spoon
paring and boning knives
small utility knife
dough scraper
hand graters, small and large
masher
garlic press
kitchen shears
rubber spatula
cooking thermometer, especially for deep-frying
kitchen scale
ruler
cheesecloth

Kitchens these days have electric mixers and food processors. Some fillings can be mixed in either and some slicing can be done in a food processor, if desired. But I prefer the control that I can exert with the hand and the cleaver. It is the traditional way, the way the finest Chinese chefs follow, and that which I recommend.

The Techniques

Let us begin with two premises: One, virtually everybody *loves* Chinese food. Two, virtually everybody *knows* that to prepare it is most difficult, too time-consuming, that the culinary world of the wok and the cleaver is not for the non-Chinese. Well, the first premise is true; the second is nonsense.

Learning to cook in the Chinese manner is not difficult. I have taught many people to cook everything from perfectly boiled rice to Peking Duck. It is true that Chinese food of all regions and of all varieties can be enjoyed in restaurants today, but that should be no excuse for not learning what is surely one of the most creative and varied cuisines in the world. Not to learn it at home is to cheat yourself out of the satisfaction and well-being that come with creation. Chinese cookery, perhaps more than any other, is constantly changing, being added to, being altered by the creativity of its practitioners. It is a living cuisine.

Really, it is not mysterious; it only has to be learned, and learning the techniques of Chinese cooking will be anything but tedious. What you will experience instead is delight.

Nor should you be awed by the idea of preparing a

banquet of several courses. Dishes can be prepared ahead, or those requiring less preparation can be paired with those needing more. The fun is in the challenge. The delight is in the eating. It seems to me that a few hours spent to prepare something that will be both beautiful to contemplate and delicious to taste is time well spent. I remember my grandmother telling me as a little girl, when my father was teaching me to cook: "In the kitchen, a little patience goes a long way." It is true. When you have created something that brings joy and smiles of satisfaction to the faces of those who are enjoying your efforts, is that not a wonderful reward? I think so.

This is the sort of feeling I have tried to transmit to my students through the years. It is not just biting into tea-smoked duck; I always say, that is delicious; but the process itself should be delicious: the preparation, the different aromas of eight-star anise, cinnamon, scallions, and ginger; the smokiness of Long Jin tea as the duck is suffused by it—these are as wonderful as the taste of the finished duck itself.

The key to this enjoyment is to do things correctly, of course, and with economy. Ingredients and utensils must be prepared. Any cookery can become overpowering and frustrating if you are ill-prepared, and Chinese cuisine, which demands a certain discipline, is no exception, but it can be relatively free of most concerns if you attend to basics. Basics means not only familiarizing yourself with different vegetables, sauces, and spices, but learning their properties and the techniques to be used with them. It also means learning the capacities of the tools necessary to work with these foods.

Cooking with the Wok

There is nothing more traditional in Chinese cookery than the wok, a thousand-year-old Chinese creation. First it was made of iron, later of carbon steel, later of aluminum. Always it was, and is, shaped like an oversize soup plate. Its concave shape places its belly right into the flame or heat source of a stove and makes it the ideal cooker for stir-frying, panfrying, deep-frying, steaming, blanching. It is perfect for sauces as well.

In carbon steel it is as perfect as can be as a cooking utensil. Though it is not a pot nor a pan, it functions as both. Its shape permits foods to be stir-fried, tossed quickly through tiny amounts of oil so that the foods cook and do not retain oiliness. The shape permits you to make the wok into a steamer simply by placing bamboo steamers in its well. Wok cooking, more than any other sort these days, is natural cooking.

If you buy only one wok, it should be of carbon steel. Avoid those with nonstick finishes because they cannot be coated with oil properly. Avoid plug-in electric woks because you cannot control heat as precisely as you must. Stainless-steel and aluminum woks are fine for steaming but cannot compare in versatility with the carbon-steel wok.

A wok of carbon steel is not pretty when it is new, because of its coating of heavy, sticky oil, but once cleaned and seasoned it is ideal and will last for years. As I wrote earlier, woks come in many sizes, but one 14 inches in diameter is the perfect all-purpose size.

Once purchased, the wok should be washed in extremely hot water with a little liquid detergent. The interior should be cleaned with a sponge, outside with steel wool and cleanser; then it should be rinsed and, while wet, placed over a flame and dried with a paper towel to prevent instant rust. With the wok still over a burner, 1 teaspoon of peanut oil should be tipped into its bowl and rubbed around with a paper towel. This oiling should be repeated until the towel is free of any traces of black residue. Your wok is now ready.

What I usually do with a new wok is make a batch of French-fried potatoes in it. That is the perfect way to season it. I pour in 4 cups of peanut oil, heat the wok until I see wisps of white smoke rising, then put in the potatoes.

After that first washing, detergents should *never* be used in the bowl of the wok. It should be washed with extremely hot water, perhaps with a stiff-bristled wok brush (inexpensive and available usually where you buy your wok) or a sponge. After rinsing, it should be dried quickly with a paper towel, then placed over a flame for a thorough drying. If you have finished cooking in it for the day, then it should be reseasoned with a bit of peanut oil rubbed around inside with a paper towel. Do this for the first 15 to 20 uses, until it becomes shiny and dark-colored, which indicates that it is completely seasoned.

If the wok is to be used several times in the course of one cooking session, then it should be washed, wiped with a towel, and dried over heat after each use.

The carbon-steel spatula you use with your wok requires the same care.

Stir-Frying

This is certainly the most dramatic of all Chinese cooking techniques. It is fascinating to watch finely sliced and chopped foods being whisked through a touch of oil and tossed with a spatula. Hands and arms move, the wok is often tipped back and forth. Stir-frying is all movement, all rhythm. What leads to it is all preparation.

The object of stir-frying is to cook vegetables precisely to the point at which they retain their flavor, color, crispness, and nutritive values. Meat is generally shredded or thinly sliced and seared so that its juices are retained. To do this you must prepare all of the ingredients of the recipe before stir-frying.

All vegetables, thinly and evenly cut, must be next to the wok, ready to be tipped into the hot oil, and so must the meat and shellfish that will accompany them. This is simply organization, so that as you cook you will have everything within reach and the rhythm of stir-frying will not be interrupted. The best stir-fried foods are those that retain their natural characteristics while at the same time absorbing and retaining the heat from the wok.

To Stir-Fry

Heat the wok for 45 seconds to 1 minute, pour oil into the wok, and coat the sides by spreading oil with a spatula. Drop a slice of ginger into the oil; when it becomes light brown, the oil is ready. (When cooking vegetables I usually add a little salt to the oil, but not when cooking meat or fish, which usually have been marinated or otherwise preseasoned.) Then place the food in the wok and begin tossing it through the oil, 1 or 2 minutes for such soft vegetables as bok choy or scallions, about a minute longer for harder vegetables such as cabbage, carrots, or broccoli. Scoop out the vegetables with a spatula and they are ready to be served.

If vegetables are too wet they will not stir-fry well, so they should be patted dry with paper towels. If they are too dry, however, you may have to sprinkle a few drops of water with your hand into the wok while cooking. When water is sprinkled in this manner, steam is created, which aids the cooking process.

Meats and shellfish, particularly shrimp, generally are stir-fried for 3 to 4 minutes, until their color changes.

Stir-frying may appear initially as a rather frenzied activity, but really it isn't; the more you do it the more you will realize that it is simply establishing a cooking rhythm.

Deep-Frying

The object of deep-frying is to cook food thoroughly inside while outside it becomes golden and lightly crusty. Most foods that are to be deep-fried are first seasoned, marinated, and dipped into batter; the object of the deep-frying process is for the oil to combine with these other tastes to create new, fresh flavors.

When I wish to make my wok into a deep-fryer I heat it briefly, then pour in 4 to 6 cups of peanut oil and heat the oil to 325° to 375° F., depending upon what I am cooking.

The oil should be heated to a temperature a bit higher than that required for frying the food because, when food is placed in it, the oil temperature will drop. It drops and rises again, and I use a frying thermometer, which I leave in the oil, to help me regulate the temperature of the oil.

When the oil reaches the proper temperature, slide the food from the inside edge of the wok into the oil. Remember to keep the temperature of the oil steady by turning the heat up or down as required.

The utensil to use for moving ingredients in deep-frying is the Chinese mesh strainer. Its large surface and stout bamboo handle are ideal for removing foods from oil and straining them as well. In my view, this strainer is far more useful than a slotted spoon.

Oil-Blanching

This relatively simple cooking technique is basically a sealing process. Its aim is to seal in the flavor of vegetables, meats, and shellfish, and to retain the bright color of vegetables.

For vegetables, heat the wok, pour 3 cups of peanut oil into it, and heat to exactly 300° F. Vegetables should be added to the oil for no longer than 30 to 45 seconds, then should be removed with a Chinese strainer.

For meats and shellfish, the oil should be at 400° to 425° F. Food is placed on the mesh of the strainer and then lowered into the oil for 1 to 1½ minutes.

When foods are removed from the oil, the excess oil should be drained off and the oil-blanched foods set aside to be used as required.

Water-Blanching

Water-blanching removes water from vegetables, meats, and shellfish. For both vegetables and meats, pour 3 to 4 cups of water into the wok, add ¼ teaspoon baking soda to the water, and bring it to a boil.

For vegetables: Place in the water and bring the water

back to a boil. Immediately drain vegetables in a strainer, place them in a bowl, and run cold water over them. Drain again and squeeze out excess water with a piece of cheese-cloth. Set aside.

For meats and shellfish: Bring water to a boil. Drop in food and bring back to a boil. Remove and drain, then place the food in a bowl, run cold water over it, and let it stand for 1 minute. Drain and set aside.

Steaming

Chinese-style steaming is truly a life-giving process. The natural tastes of fish and vegetables are preserved when steamed. Doughs become soft, light, and firm breads, dumplings, and crêpes when subjected to steam's wet, penetrating heat. Food that is dry becomes moist; that which is shrunken, expands. Steaming bestows a glistening coat of moisture on foods.

It is an artful technique as well, because foods can be arranged in lovely ways within bamboo steamers, and once cooked, they can be served without being disturbed. Steaming requires virtually no oil, except that used to coat the bamboo reeds at the bottoms of the steamers, to prevent sticking. (Even a bamboo, lettuce, or cabbage leaf can be used as a liner, thus eliminating any need for oil.)

To steam, pour 4 to 5 cups of water into a wok and bring it to a boil. Place steamers in the wok so that they sit evenly above, but not touching, the water. This can be done with a cake rack. You will be able to stack two steamers, even more. Cover the top one, and the contents of all will cook beautifully. Boiling water should be on hand at all times during the steaming process, to replace any water that evaporates from the wok.

Preparing Porcelain and Pyrex for Steaming

Occasionally foods are placed within steamers in porcelain or Pyrex dishes to cook and serve on. These dishes must first be seasoned, or tempered.

Fill the wok with 5 to 6 cups of cold water. Place a cake rack inside and pile up dishes to be prepared on the rack, making certain they are completely covered by the cold water. Cover with a wok cover and bring the water to a boil. Let the water boil for 10 minutes, turn off heat, and allow the wok to cool to room temperature. The dishes are then seasoned and can be placed in steamers without fear that they will crack. They may be used in place of steamers themselves. The foods are placed in the tempered dishes, which are in turn placed on cake racks in the wok. Cover and steam as in process just described.

Cooking Rice

For many beginners the most mystifying cooking technique is preparing that basic Chinese staple—properly cooked rice. Good rice is really easy to prepare. Here is a foolproof method of cooking fine rice.

Use long-grain rice. A good ratio is 1 cup of rice to 7½ ounces of water for 2 people. So-called old rice, that which has been lying about in sacks for long periods, will absorb more water and will be easier to cook.

1.   Wash rice 3 or 4 times, 30 minutes before cooking. As you rinse it, rub it between your hands. Drain well after washing. Place in a pot, add water, and allow to rest for 2 hours before cooking.

2.   Begin cooking uncovered over high heat, stir with chopsticks, and cook for about 4 minutes. Water will evaporate and rice will remain quite hard. Cover the pot and cook over low heat for about 8 minutes more, stirring from time to time.

3.   Turn off heat and loosen rice with chopsticks. This will help retain fluffiness. Cover tightly until ready to serve. Just before serving stir rice with chopsticks once again.

Well-cooked rice will have absorbed the water but will not be lumpy, nor will the kernels stick together.

Preparing Broths (Stocks)

As you will see, in this book I often use chicken, fish, and vegetable broths as recipe ingredients. These are basically stocks, which I make myself. They are delicious additions and add measurably to the recipes. Here is how to make them:

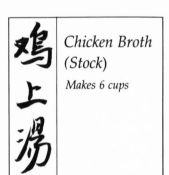

Chicken Broth (Stock)

Makes 6 cups

 7 pounds chicken bones and skin
10 cups water
 3 quarts cold water
 1 piece of fresh ginger, 1 inch thick, slightly mashed
 2 garlic cloves, whole, peeled
 4 scallions: discard ends, wash, dry, cut into halves
 2 medium-size onions; peel, quarter
   Salt to taste

1.   In a large pot, bring the 10 cups water to a boil. Add chicken bones and skin and allow to boil for 1 minute. This will bring blood and meat juices to the top. Turn off heat, pour off water, run cold water over skin and bones to clean them.

2.   Place skin and bones in a stockpot; add 3 quarts cold water, the ginger, garlic, scallions, onions, and salt to taste. Cover and bring to a boil, partially uncover, and allow broth to simmer for 3½ to 4 hours.

3.   Strain contents; reserve liquid, discard solid ingredients. Refrigerate until used.

This stock will keep for 2 to 3 days refrigerated, or it can be frozen for about 1 month.

*Fish Broth
(Stock)*

Makes 8 cups

10 pounds fish heads and bones: wash well in cold
    running water
4 quarts cold water
2 pounds onions: peel and quarter
6 scallions: discard both ends, wash, dry, cut into ½-
    inch pieces
2 slices of fresh ginger: smash lightly with cleaver, cut
    into halves
6 garlic cloves, whole, peeled
1 teaspoon white pepper

1. In a large stockpot, place all ingredients. Set over high
heat and bring to a boil. Lower heat, partially cover pot,
but keep at a boil at all times. Cook for 6 hours.

2. Turn off heat; using a large strainer over a mixing
bowl, ladle broth through strainer. Refrigerate until ready
to use.

This stock can be kept, refrigerated, for 2 to 3 days, or
it can be frozen for about a month.

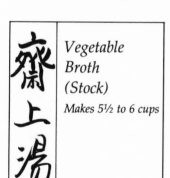

*Vegetable
Broth
(Stock)*

Makes 5½ to 6 cups

10 cups water
 3 large yellow onions, cut into quarters
 8 celery ribs, cut into thirds
 3 large carrots, cut into thirds
 ½ pound fresh mushrooms, cut into halves
 1 large piece of fresh ginger, about 1 by 2 inches
 2 teaspoons salt
 ⅛ teaspoon white pepper
 3 tablespoons scallion oil or peanut oil

1. In a large pot, bring the water to a boil. Scrub and cut
up the vegetables as described, but leave the skins on.
Add all the ingredients to the boiling water, reduce heat,
and simmer in a partially covered pot for 3½ hours.

2. When the stock is cooked, remove from heat and
strain the liquid through a metal strainer. Discard solids.
Store stock in a plastic container until needed.

This stock can be kept in the refrigerator for 4 or 5
days, or can be frozen for 3 to 4 weeks.

Working with the Cleaver

If the wok is an all-purpose cooker, then the cleaver comes close to being the all-purpose cutting instrument of the Chinese kitchen. Nobody who cooks Chinese food should be without the broad, rectangular-bladed, wood-handled cleaver. It is rather formidable looking and many beginners think dire things about it, such as that it may cut off their fingers when they begin slicing vegetables. Understandable, I suppose, but not true.

The cleaver, when held correctly, so that its weight and balance will be utilized well, can do virtually anything a handful of lesser knives can. It slices, shreds, threads, dices, cubes, chops, minces, and hacks, all with great ease. It mashes, it is a scoop, it can be a dough scraper.

Cleavers come in various sizes and weights, some about ¾ pound, which are fine for slicing and cutting; heavier sorts of about 1 pound, which are better for mincing; and still heavier cleavers of about 2 pounds, which will chop through any meat and all but the heaviest bones. If you are to have but a single all-purpose cleaver, I recommend one that weighs about 1 pound, is about 8 inches long, and has a blade 3½ to 3¾ inches wide.

Different people hold cleavers in different ways, and that is perfectly fine, for, despite the belief that there is a "proper" way to hold them, there is really no single way to do so. Above all it should be held comfortably and in such a way as to make its weight and its blade work efficiently.

I use three basic grips.

The first, for chopping and mincing: I grip the handle in a fistlike grasp and swing it straight down. The stroke will be long and forceful if I am cutting bone or a substance that is quite thick. If I am mincing, the strokes will be short, rapid, and controlled. The wrist dictates the force.

The second, for slicing, shredding, and dicing: I grip the handle as before, but permit the index finger to stretch out along the side of the flat blade to give it guidance. The wrist, which barely moves with this grip, is virtually rigid and almost becomes an extension of the cleaver, as the blade is drawn across the food to be cut. When you use this grip, your other hand becomes a guide. Your finger-tips should anchor the food to be cut and your knuckle joints should guide the cleaver blade, which will brush them ever so slightly as it moves across the food.

Vegetables and meats are sliced, shredded, or diced. Garlic, occasionally ginger, and shrimp are generally minced.

The third, for removing gristle from meat or peeling vegetables: I grip the handle tightly, with my thumb and index finger holding both sides of the flat of the blade. The cleaver is almost horizontal. Then, as the free hand lifts pieces of gristle away from meats and fowl, the cleaver blade is gently inserted and follows the hand, cutting the gristle as the hand lifts it. When peeling, as with water chestnuts, the cleaver is steady; the free hand manipulates what is to be peeled.

A cleaver, because it is made of carbon steel, should be washed and dried quickly to prevent rust. Under no circumstances should it be placed in a dishwasher. If your cleaver should show a spot of rust, it should be rubbed with steel wool, dried, and touched with a bit of vegetable oil.

Slicing

Mashing

Cubing

Dicing

Boning Fowl

Most people believe that to bone a duck or a chicken is virtually an impossible task. This is not so. I have taught dozens of students to bone ducks and chickens perfectly, without so much as piercing their skins. There are two recipes in this book that call for the procedure, one a recipe for Eight-Jewel Stuffed Duck, a Hakka preparation, the other a specialty of New Year's, Kwangtung Crisp Stuffed Chicken. The method for boning the duck is quite clear and precise (see page 169); the same procedure should be followed with the chicken.

Cutting Up Fowl

Sit bird up, its back to you, its tail portion down. Using a cleaver, cut downward from the spinal joint. When you have cut through, use your hands to pull the chicken apart. With cleaver cut the center joint of the breast bone. The bird is now cut into halves. Cut off the thighs and wings at their joints. Cut each half of the body into halves lengthwise, then cut these lengths into bite-size pieces.

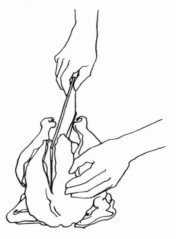

Sit the bird up, its back to you. Using a cleaver, cut downward from the spinal joint.

When you have cut through, use your hands to pull the chicken apart.

With a cleaver cut the center joint of the breastbone.

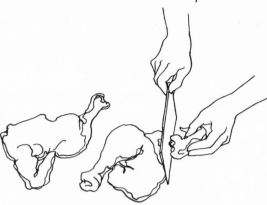

Cut off the thighs and the wings at their joints.

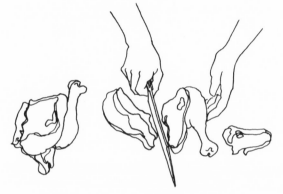

Cut each piece in half lengthwise.

Cut these pieces into smaller bite-sized pieces.

The Art of Vegetable Sculpture

Experienced Chinese chefs, particularly those of Suzhou near Shanghai, those in Shanghai itself, in Peking, and in Chiu Chow below Canton, have a long tradition of carving vegetables to be used as elaborate, decorative garnishes. They carve melons, turnips, radishes, carrots, tomatoes, and eggplants into all sorts of fanciful birds and beasts. We can't all be master culinary sculptors of course, but there are a few simple food carvings that you can do that will enhance your banquet platters. Here are a few, with directions on how to carve them.

Lobster

Use a cucumber, the greenest and firmest available.

1.   Cut a large cucumber to a piece about 6 inches long, preserving the rounded end. Cut into halves lengthwise. Sculpt the tail: Make a large notch about 2 inches from the rounded end on either side. Cut tiny scallops or notches in the rounded end to create a jagged edge. Starting from the cut end, cut 3 thin "flaps" about ⅛ inch wide, extending to about ¼ inch from the large notch. Do not cut the flaps off; leave them attached at lower end.

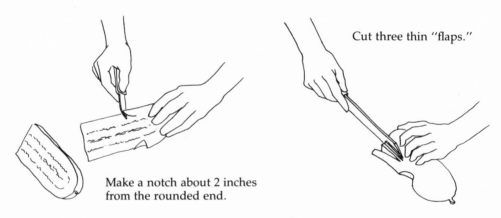

Cut three thin "flaps."

Make a notch about 2 inches from the rounded end.

2.   To shape the head: Create the pointed sawtooth edge, about 3 or 4 "teeth" per side. Notch the center piece all around to create a jagged lobster "head." Cut tiny notches along either side of the center lobster "head." Slide your knife under each notch so that they will curl up.

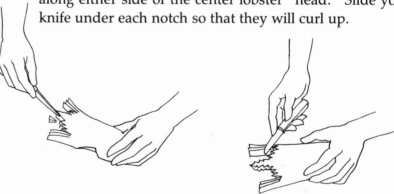

Cut shallow slits down the back.

3. Cut shallow slits down the back or "thorax" of the lobster. At the tail end, cut slits 1 inch in length in a fan-shaped design, extending from the tail toward the upper back.

4. To finish: Roll the inner flaps over and tuck them in, forming a curl. To create eyes, take 2 red kitchen matches, cut off ends, and push match wood into the lobster's head.

The finished lobster

Crab
Use a medium to large cucumber, dark green in color and firm.

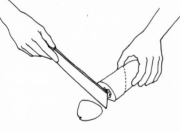

Cut a 4-inch section from the center of a cucumber.

1. Cut a 4-inch section from the center of the cucumber, then cut it into halves lengthwise. At both ends slice off pieces on the diagonal, making certain the cuts are at opposite angles.

2. Cut 3 thin flaps on either side of the crab's body. Make sure that the slices are very thin so that they will not break off. If they are too wide, they will break off easily and will resist being curled.

Cut three thin flaps on either side of the crab's body.

3.   To form the claws: Cut a triangle out of the wide part of the body, with the point of the triangle at the center front. The two claws will be formed. Take a small slice out of the outer edge of each claw. Make a notch in the center of each claw. Make tiny notches around the carving between the claws.

4.   To finish: Curl the flaps over and tuck in. Form eyes, using red ends of kitchen matches.

To form the claws, cut a triangle out of the wide part of the body.

To finish, curl the flaps over and tuck in.

Ferns
Use a firm, green cucumber.

1.   Cut the end off a cucumber, about 3 inches in length. Slice the end piece lengthwise, about ½ to ¾ inch wide.

2.   Make a series of very thin slices into the piece, ending about ½ inch from the rounded end. When you have finished the slicing, press the side of your cleaver down gently onto the whole piece, making the thin slices fan out. This makes a simple, and tasty, decoration.

Cauliflower Ferns

These are made from a cauliflower stalk. Cut the stalk into long, thin sheaves. Along each sheaf, make small fringed cuts. When the sheaf is dropped into cold water it will bend and separate, forming a simple and beautiful decoration.

Turnip Flowers

Use a somewhat narrow white turnip, or Chinese turnip.

1. Cut a piece of turnip about 1½ inches wide. Around the outer edge, slice a row of petals by slicing from top to bottom into, but not through, the bottom of the turnip piece.

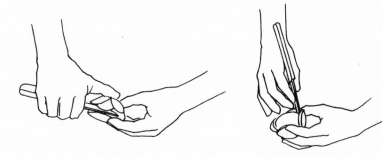

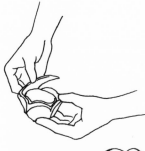

2. Then cut a ridge in the center of the turnip piece all the way through. Discard the piece.

3. Begin the second row of petals, positioning the second row of petals alternately between the petals of the first row.

4. Repeat the process of cutting and discarding ridges, and making petals until you have 4 rows.

Carrot Flowerets

Use the thicker end, the leaf end, of a rather large carrot. Cut the end off, peel it, and carve the end into a pointed cone.

With a very sharp paring knife, pare along the cone's surface, shaving a continuous slice. Go twice around the cone, then a bit more. Remove, take both ends, and curl them together to create a figure-eight floweret. The same process may be used to create Zucchini Flowerets, but do not peel the skin before paring. These should be kept in cold water, refrigerated, until used.

Carve the thick end of a carrot into a pointed cone.

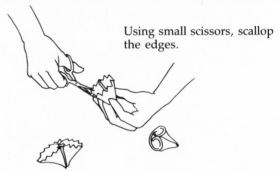

Using small scissors, scallop the edges.

Scallion Flowers

Use rather large scallions for these, preferably those with bulbous white portions.

Break off whiskers; do not cut, so base remains intact. Cut petal-like shapes into the bulb of the scallion, rather deeply into the body. Cut around until you have cut 4 or

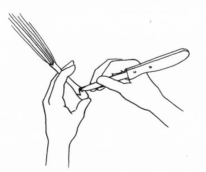

Cut petallike shapes into the bulb of the scallion.

Pull the stalk out of the bulb.

5 petals with tips facing up toward green portion. Then hold bulb in one hand and with other pull the stalk out. It should come out easily because it has been cut through. Separate the petals with your fingers gently. Soak in cold water until the petals open. Keep refrigerated in cold water until used.

Turnip Basket

Use a rather large white turnip for this, preferably one at least 3 inches in diameter.

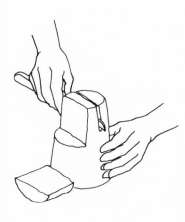

1.   Cut a cylindrical piece out of turnip, 4½ inches long. Stand it on end and cut a basket shape and handle, as illustrated.

2.   Beginning at bottom, cut a row of small petals around the base. Then cut a row of larger petals. Break off this second row and discard. Cut another row. Cut another row and discard. Repeat process until you have 3 rows of petals in ascending sizes, with 2 rows between them that have been broken off.

3.   Carve the trunk of the turnip into 2 points, one on each side of the basket in a way that puts the points in a line crossing the handle of the basket; discard turnip around them.

4.   Hollow out center of turnip. Make tiny notches along the edges of the handle. The basket can be used to hold tiny flowers and vegetables as garnishes. Keep in cold water, refrigerated, until used.

Beginning at bottom, shape small petals around the base.

Hollow out center and make notches along the edges of the handle.

Eating the Chinese Way

There is of course only *one* way to hold chopsticks properly. Once you have learned all the other techniques, you should master that as well.

There is also a proper way to hold a rice bowl, a proper way to hold a soup bowl, as well as those small porcelain soup spoons.

It now becomes time to cook, to eat, to enjoy.

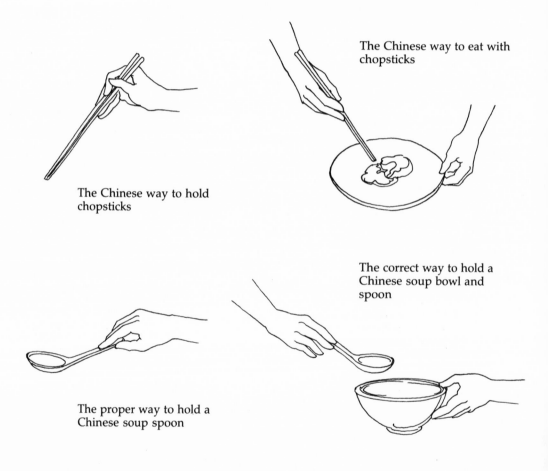

The Chinese way to eat with chopsticks

The Chinese way to hold chopsticks

The correct way to hold a Chinese soup bowl and spoon

The proper way to hold a Chinese soup spoon

The Regional Feasts

A COLD BANQUET

GAI YAU DONG GU	*Steamed Black Mushrooms*
TIENTSIN LOT BOK CHOY	*Spicy Tientsin Cabbage*
YUEN SEE CHAU HAR	*Marinated Shrimp in Brown Bean Sauce*
CHING PING GAI	*Boiled Chicken, Ching Ping Market Style*
PONG PONG GAI	*Hacked Chicken*
CHAR SIU	*Roast Pork*
NG HEUNG NGAU YUK	*Five-Spice Beef*
WOR MEI DZI GEUNG	*Ginger Pickle*
TIM HOP TOH	*Honey Walnuts*

The First Course

Throughout China, it is customary to begin all banquets with foods prepared to be served at room temperature. These *ping poon,* or appetizers, can be as simple as individual plates of steamed black mushrooms, pickled ginger, or honey walnuts; or as elaborate as storks and egrets carved from white turnips; lanterns hollowed out of wintermelons; birds, dragons, and phoenixes in relief, on plates, created from layers of sliced chicken, beef, vegetables, and shrimp.

These appetizers are universal. Though they began as recipes from China's various regions, they now are served, interchangeably, throughout the country.

The *ping poon* here can be used as the first part of a *bat dai, bat siu* banquet, about which I wrote earlier; any one of them can be the first course of one of the regional banquets that follow; or you can even create a "cold" banquet of the nine appetizers themselves. What a wonderful summer banquet that would be!

| GAI YAU DONG GU |
| Steamed Black Mushrooms |

24 silver-dollar-sized dried Chinese black mushrooms
½ teaspoon salt
1 teaspoon sugar
½ teaspoon dark soy sauce
2 scallions: discard ends, wash, dry, cut into 2-inch slices
1 ounce raw chicken fat: cut into 2 pieces
1 slice of fresh ginger: smash with cleaver blade

1.   Soak the mushrooms in hot water for 1 hour. Wash thoroughly and squeeze out the excess water. Remove the stems and place the mushrooms in a heatproof dish.

2.   Add the salt, sugar, and soy sauce to the dish and toss with mushrooms.

3.   On top of the mushrooms, place the scallions, chicken fat, and ginger. In a steamer steam them for 30 minutes.

4.   Turn off heat, remove from steamer. Discard scallions, ginger, and chicken fat and gently toss mushrooms in remaining liquid. Allow to cool to room temperature. Cover with plastic wrap and refrigerate until used.

❧ *These will keep refrigerated for 4 to 5 days. Serve at slightly cooler than room temperature.*

| TIENTSIN LOT BOK CHOY |
| Spicy Tientsin Cabbage |

2 pounds Tientsin cabbage, white portions only: wash and dry thoroughly (10 cups tightly packed)
1½ teaspoons salt
½ cup sweet red pepper: cut into ¼-inch julienne
3 tablespoons white vinegar
2 tablespoons sugar
1½ teaspoons sesame oil
½ teaspoon hot oil
2 tablespoons corn oil
10 small dried hot chili peppers

1. Cut cabbage stalks diagonally at ¼-inch intervals. Place in a large bowl. Sprinkle with salt and mix thoroughly with hands. Allow to stand, covered, overnight in refrigerator.

2. Drain off liquid. Add sliced sweet pepper, white vinegar, sugar, sesame oil, and hot oil. Toss together in the bowl. Set aside.

3. Heat wok for 1 minute. Add corn oil; heat until hot, about 30 seconds. Add dried hot chili peppers; stir until peppers turn quite dark. Turn heat off. Pour entire contents of wok into bowl of cabbage and mix all with hands.

4. Refrigerate, covered, for 8 hours or overnight.

❦ *Spicy Tientsin Cabbage will keep for 1 to 2 weeks refrigerated.*

YUEN
SEE
CHAU
HAR

Marinated Shrimp in Brown Bean Sauce

1 pound medium shrimp, 26 to 30: shell, devein, wash, dry thoroughly

For marinade, combine in a bowl and mix well:
  2 teaspoons dark soy sauce
  2 tablespoons oyster sauce
  1 teaspoon sesame oil
1½ teaspoons sugar
  ½ teaspoon grated ginger
  1 teaspoon white wine

2½ to 3 tablespoons peanut oil
1½ teaspoons minced ginger
  1 tablespoon brown bean sauce
  1 tablespoon white wine
  2 to 3 scallions, finely chopped

1. Marinate shrimp for 30 minutes. Drain through a strainer, but reserve liquid.

2. Heat a wok. Add peanut oil. When a wisp of white smoke appears, add minced ginger. Coat wok with a spatula, add brown bean sauce, mix.

3. Over high heat add shrimp. Spread in a thin layer, tipping wok from side to side to spread heat evenly. Turn over. Add wine around edges. Toss together well. If too dry add a bit of marinade. When shrimp turn pink they are done.

4. Turn off heat. Add chopped scallions and toss with shrimp. Remove from wok and place in a dish. Allow to cool to room temperature. Cover with plastic wrap and refrigerate. Serve cool.

❧ *I do not recommend preparing this dish too far in advance. It is best when eaten the same day it is prepared.*

CHING PING GAI

Boiled Chicken, Ching Ping Market Style

In Canton there is a wonderful fresh food market, called Ching Ping, which cuts through a series of narrow streets in the middle of the city. It is filled with fresh vegetables and fruits, all kinds of live fish and poultry, as well as an enormous variety of prepared foods. On a recent trip to Canton I discovered this recipe by accident. I had stopped to look at an array of cooked and barbecued chickens, ducks, and geese, and was given a taste. What was this? I asked. Ching Pin Gai, I was told. I asked the man in the market how it was made and he told me. Here it is.

8 cups cold water
6 basil leaves, fresh preferred
6 mint leaves, fresh preferred

2 scallions: discard both ends, wash, cut into halves
2 cinnamon sticks
1 large slice of fresh ginger
¼ cup Shao-Hsing Rice Wine (I prefer this brand from the People's Republic of China. If unavailable use sherry.)
2 ounces sugar cane sugar, or ¼ cup brown sugar
4 teaspoons salt
1 whole chicken, 3 pounds: remove all fat and membranes and wash inside and out; allow all water to drain off

1.   In a large oval Dutch oven place the 8 cups water. Add all ingredients except chicken. Bring to a boil and allow to boil for 5 minutes.

2.   Lower heat. Place chicken, breast side up, in liquid. Return to a boil. Reduce heat, partially cover oven, and allow chicken to simmer for 15 minutes.

3.   Turn chicken over and allow to simmer for an additional 15 minutes. Turn off heat and allow chicken to sit in liquid for 5 minutes more.

4.   Remove chicken from liquid; allow to cool to room temperature. Place in a dish, cover with plastic wrap, and refrigerate. Slice when cold, and serve.

NOTE: This recipe carries with it a bonus. There should be about 8 cups of liquid remaining after cooking, and it is a perfect base for egg drop soup. Simply bring it to a boil, after straining it, and gradually pour in 6 beaten eggs as you beat the soup with a cooking fork. It will yield 10 servings of soup. Garnish with ¼ cup of finely sliced green portions of scallions.

❧ *Ching Ping Chicken will keep refrigerated for 3 to 4 days. It cannot be frozen.*

PONG
PONG
GAI

Hacked Chicken

2 whole 1-pound chicken breasts
8 cups water
4 scallions: wash, discard both ends, cut into halves
1 teaspoon salt
2 teaspoons sugar
1 slice of ginger, ¼ inch thick
2 garlic cloves, peeled
1½ cups shredded lettuce, for garnish

For sauce, combine in a bowl and mix well:
2½ tablespoons peanut butter
2½ tablespoons dark soy sauce
5½ tablespoons chicken broth
2½ teaspoons sugar
4½ teaspoons white vinegar
2½ teaspoons minced garlic
1½ teaspoons minced ginger
2½ teaspoons hot oil
  5 teaspoons sesame oil
1½ teaspoons Shao-Hsing wine or sherry
4½ tablespoons finely sliced scallions

1.   Place the chicken in a large pot with the water and add scallions, salt, sugar, ginger, and garlic. Bring to a boil over high heat. Then lower heat and partially cover the pot. Cook for about 25 minutes.

2.   Remove chicken from the pot and place in a bowl with enough cold water to cover chicken. This will stop the cooking. Let it sit for 5 minutes.

3.   Remove chicken from bowl and place in refrigerator to cool for 3 hours.

4.   Remove chicken from refrigerator. Take off skin and fat and break breast into halves, removing the bone. Place chicken on a chopping board and beat it with a rolling pin or wooden dowel to break the fiber. Tear the meat into shredded strips with your fingers.

5. Spread shredded lettuce on a serving dish. Place shredded chicken atop it and pour sauce over chicken. Serve immediately.

An arrangement of cold meats

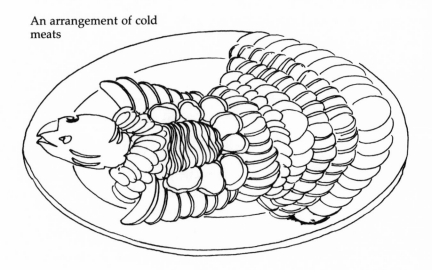

| CHAR SIU |
| Roast Pork |

4½ pounds lean pork butt

For marinade, combine in a bowl and mix well:
3 tablespoons dark soy sauce
3 tablespoons light soy sauce
3 tablespoons honey
½ teaspoon salt
3 tablespoons oyster sauce
2 tablespoons blended whiskey
3 tablespoons hoisin sauce
⅛ teaspoon white pepper
½ cake wet preserved bean curd (*see note*)
1 teaspoon five-spice powder

1. Cut the pork into strips 1 inch thick. Using a small knife, pierce the meat repeatedly at ½-inch intervals to help tenderize it.

2. Line a roasting pan with foil. Place the strips of meat in a single layer at the bottom of the roasting pan.

3. Pour the marinade over the meat, and allow to marinate for 4 hours or overnight.

4. Preheat the oven to broil. Place the roasting pan in the oven and roast the pork for 30 to 50 minutes. To test, remove one strip of pork after 30 minutes and slice it to see if it is cooked through. During the cooking period, meat should be basted 5 or 6 times and turned 4 times. If the sauce dries out, add water to the pan.

5. When the meat is cooked, allow it to cool, then refrigerate it until you are ready to use it.

NOTE: Wet preserved bean curd comes in both cans and jars. The canned bean curds are larger than those that come in jars. If you use the canned curds, only half a cake is required for this recipe; if you use the curds in jars, use 2 small cakes.

❧ *Char Siu can be made ahead. It can be refrigerated for 4 to 5 days, and it can be frozen for 1 month. Allow it to defrost before using.*

NG
HEUNG
NGAU
YUK

Five-Spice Beef

6 cups cold water
3½ to 4 pounds shin of beef
6 ounces sugar cane sugar or brown sugar
½ cup white wine
2 garlic cloves, whole
2 slices of ginger
3 cinnamon sticks
3 pieces of 8-star anise (whole flower)
¼ teaspoon Szechuan peppercorns
1 teaspoon salt
¾ cup dark soy sauce (to be added when water boils)

1. Pour cold water into a large pot. Add all other ingredients except dark soy sauce.

2. Bring to a boil, add dark soy sauce, return to a boil. Reduce heat and simmer beef for 3 to 4 hours. Leave cover off, but if water seems to be evaporating too quickly, place cover partially on top, leaving space for steam to escape. Turn meat occasionally.

3. Use a chopstick to test the beef. When the chopstick goes into the meat easily, it is done. There should be about 2½ cups of cooking liquid remaining. Turn off heat. Cover pot and allow to cool to room temperature.

4. Place meat in a shallow dish. Discard cooking liquid. Cover meat with plastic wrap and refrigerate. When the meat is cooled it can be sliced and served.

❧ *Five-Spice Beef can be kept refrigerated for 5 to 7 days. It can be frozen for 6 to 8 weeks, but it must be placed in a container to which 1½ cups of the cooking liquid have been added. Allow to defrost before slicing.*

WOR
MEI
DZI
GEUNG

Ginger Pickle

6 cups water
½ teaspoon baking soda
1¼ pounds young, fresh ginger: peel, wash, dry, slice
     thinly

For marinade, combine in a bowl and mix well:
  1 teaspoon salt
  2 tablespoons white vinegar
  6 tablespoons sugar

1.   In a large pot bring water and baking soda to a boil. Add ginger and boil for 30 seconds to 1 minute. Remove from flame. Add cold water to reduce temperature. Drain. Add cold water a second time and drain. Repeat a third time. Drain well, then place ginger in a bowl.

2.   Add marinade to ginger. Mix well. Cover and refrigerate for at least 24 hours before serving.

NOTE: Ginger placed in a tightly closed jar will keep, in the refrigerator, for at least 3 months.

    Young ginger is occasionally difficult to obtain. It is available only twice each year, in late spring and late fall. Ginger pickle is also available prepared in jars.

甜核桃

TIM
HOP
TOH

*Honey
Walnuts*

4 to 5 cups water
12 ounces freshly shelled walnuts
1½ ounces sugar
6 tablespoons water (to make sugar glaze)
3 to 4 cups peanut oil

1. Bring 4 to 5 cups water to a boil in a wok.

2. Place walnuts in boiling water for 5 minutes to remove bitter taste. Remove from water and drain, then run cold water over walnuts. Drain again, then place back in the wok with another 4 cups water.

3. Bring to a boil and cook for another 5 minutes. Repeat draining process. Set aside and let drain.

4. Wash wok. Add 6 tablespoons water and bring to a boil. Then add sugar, constantly stirring. Let boil for 1 minute. Add walnuts. Stir until walnuts are coated with sugar and remaining liquid in wok has evaporated.

5. Remove walnuts and set aside. Wash wok with extremely hot water to remove sugar. Dry.

6. Place peanut oil in wok. Bring to a boil (look for a wisp of white smoke), then add walnuts. Fry for 4 to 5 minutes, until walnuts turn golden brown.

❧ *Honey Walnuts can be frozen for 3 to 4 weeks.*

A BANQUET FROM CANTON

GAU CHOI SOI GAU — *Water Dumplings with Chives*

HAR LUNG WU — *Shrimp with Lobster Sauce*

SEE JIU CHAU NGAU — *Pepper Steak*

SEUN MOI OP — *Steamed Duck with Preserved Plums*

SZE GUA TONG — *Silk Squash Soup with Shredded Pork*

LING MUNG GAI — *Lemon Chicken*

WU LO YUK — *Sweet and Sour Pork*

SING JAU CHAU MAI FUN — *Singapore Noodles*

JING SEK BON — *Steamed Sea Bass*

南方粤菜 CANTON
Cooking of the South

Perhaps the most familiar of Chinese regional cuisines is Cantonese. Canton is the home of black beans, cured pork sausages, pressed and cured ducks and geese, the roast pork known as *char siu*, roast pig, and steamed fish. It is where stir-frying and steaming are high art, where dim sum, those small dumplings that "dot the heart," originated. It is also the most varied of all of the cuisines of China, a consequence of many factors.

Canton is China's richest growing area, a subtropical bowl that produces tons and tons of rice and vegetables and fruits including oranges, tangerines, pineapples, and coconuts. Its waters account for one quarter of the country's total seafood catch and its offshore fish farms abound with prawns and grouper. Canton thus has had the raw materials with which to experiment, to change an existing cuisine. It is also the region which has been most open to Western influences—and even today is the heart of East-West trade—so that such concepts as roasting beef, currying lamb, even making ice cream, came early to Canton.

The essence of the Cantonese kitchen is freshness. A duck or a chicken should be alive when selected in the market; vegetables should be just minutes off the vine, or out of the ground. Fish should be swimming. The way food is cooked in Canton emphasizes that freshness. Vegetables lose none of their crispness since they are whisked quickly through small amounts of oil. With its almost instant cooking, its high-heat stir-frying, its *wok hai*, no cookery anywhere can match it for retention of natural flavors and textures. Fish are firm and plump when properly steamed. Often called bland, Cantonese cooking is certainly the most sophisticated of all Chinese cuisines, easily comparable to classic French cookery in its uses of spices and flavorings. It is a cuisine that demands the complete attention of your palate.

Because its tastes are so varied, so subtle, great care is exerted to orchestrate a banquet, not only in Canton, but everywhere in China. The taste of one dish should naturally follow that of its predecessor, naturally introduce its successor. Tastes should escalate from the mild to the spicy, then the palate should be cleansed and the tastes should deescalate. It is challenging to arrange foods that way in a banquet, but so satisfying.

GAU
CHOI
SOI
GAU

*Water
Dumplings
with Chives*

Makes 45 dumplings

2¼ cups chives: wash, dry, cut into ¼-inch lengths
 1 tablespoon peanut oil
1⅛ teaspoons salt
10 ounces shrimp
12 ounces ground pork
 1 teaspoon grated ginger mixed with 1 teaspoon white
     wine
1½ teaspoons sugar
1½ teaspoons sesame oil
 1 teaspoon peanut oil
 1 teaspoon light soy sauce
1½ tablespoons oyster sauce
 2 tablespoons cornstarch
     Pinch of white pepper
45 won ton skins
 1 egg, beaten
 5 cups chicken broth
 1 cup cold water
 1 cup chives, cut into ¼-inch lengths, for soup

1.   Stir-fry chives in 1 tablespoon peanut oil with ⅛ teaspoon salt until chives change color. Reserve.

2.   Shell and devein shrimp. Wash and dry thoroughly. Dice into ⅛-inch cubes.

3.   In the bowl of an electric mixer, combine 2 cups chives, shrimp, pork, ginger, remaining salt, and next 7 ingredients. Blend evenly and thoroughly. Refrigerate for 4 hours.

4.   Using kitchen scissors, cut won ton skins into circular pieces 2¼ inches in diameter.

5.   Place 1½ to 2 teaspoons of filling in the center of each skin. With a butter knife, brush egg around the outer edge of the skin. Fold skin in half-moon shape and press together tightly with thumb and forefinger to seal.

6. Cook dumplings in 3 quarts boiling water for 5 to 7 minutes. Run cold water over cooked dumplings and drain.

7. In a pot bring chicken broth and cold water to a boil. Add remaining ¼ cup of the chives. Add dumplings. Turn off heat and serve immediately.

NOTE: If you do not have an electric mixer, mix ingredients thoroughly with two pairs of chopsticks or a wooden spoon, stirring clockwise until consistency is smooth and even.

HAR
LUNG
WU

Shrimp with Lobster Sauce

My students ask, "Where is the lobster?" and I explain that in Cantonese cuisine "lobster sauce" means the sauce that you prepare for lobster, not a sauce made with lobster. It would be clearer, but not as rhythmic, I suppose, to call this "shrimp with the sauce that is used for lobster." It doesn't scan.

1 pound shrimp

For shrimp marinade, combine in a bowl and mix well:
  1 teaspoon light soy sauce
  ½ tablespoon white wine mixed with ½ teaspoon
     ginger juice
  ½ tablespoon oyster sauce
  ½ to 1 teaspoon sesame oil
  ½ teaspoon salt
  1 teaspoon sugar
  2 teaspoons cornstarch
    Pinch of white pepper

4 ounces ground pork

For pork marinade, combine in a bowl:
¼ teaspoon light soy sauce
½ teaspoon oyster sauce
¼ teaspoon salt
¼ teaspoon cornstarch

2 eggs
3 tablespoons peanut oil
2 garlic cloves, minced
1 slice of ginger
¼ cup chicken broth (to be used to thin sauce, if
     necessary)
1½ scallions, finely sliced
Several sprigs of coriander or parsley

1. Shell and devein shrimp. Wash in salt water, drain thoroughly, and dry with a paper towel. Place shrimp in shrimp marinade; set aside. Add ground pork to pork marinade; set aside. Beat eggs.

2. Heat a wok over high heat; add 1 tablespoon peanut oil with 1 minced garlic clove. When garlic browns, add pork mixture. Stir-fry until meat turns from pink to white.

3. Add beaten eggs to pork mixture and stir together until the mixture is softly scrambled. Remove the mixture and reserve. Remove wok from the stove, wash and dry completely, and replace on stove.

4. Heat the wok over high heat; add 2 tablespoons peanut oil with the slice of ginger and remaining minced garlic clove. When garlic turns brown, add shrimp in a single layer. Turn wok from side to side over heat to cook evenly. Turn shrimp over and mix; stir-fry until shrimp turn pink.

5. Add pork-egg mixture and stir together for about 1 minute. If sauce is overly thick, add chicken broth, a little at a time. Turn off heat and remove. Place in a serving dish, sprinkle scallion on top, and place coriander or parsley sprigs on the side to garnish.

SEE
JIU
CHAU
NGAU

Pepper Steak

This dish illustrates the essence of what the Cantonese call *Wok Hai* cookery, stir-frying over extremely high heat, with the black-bean and garlic paste sending out an utterly wonderful aroma. My daughter claims that she smelled Pepper Steak cooking two blocks away from our house, while en route home from school one day.

12 ounces "oyster cut" London broil

For marinade, combine in a bowl and mix well:
 1 tablespoon whiskey mixed with 1 teaspoon ginger juice
 1 teaspoon dark soy sauce
 ½ teaspoon sesame oil
 1½ teaspoons oyster sauce
 ½ teaspoon salt
 1 teaspoon sugar
 1½ teaspoons cornstarch
  Pinch of white pepper

12 ounces fresh green peppers
 2 tablespoons black beans
 2 garlic cloves
 3 tablespoons peanut oil
 1 slice of fresh ginger

For sauce, combine in a bowl and mix well:
 ½ tablespoon oyster sauce
 ½ cup cold water
 1 teaspoon dark soy sauce
 1 tablespoon cornstarch
 ¼ teaspoon sugar
 ¼ teaspoon salt
  Pinch of white pepper

1. Cut beef across the grain into thin slices 1 by 2½ inches, and place in the marinade. Wash, seed, and dry peppers and cut into thin slices, ¼ by 2½ inches. Wash and drain black beans and mash them into a paste. Mince the 2 garlic cloves and add them to the black beans.

2.   Heat a wok over high heat, add 1 tablespoon peanut oil and a slice of ginger, and stir-fry the peppers for just under 1 minute. Remove from wok and set aside. Remove wok from stove, wash and dry completely, and return to stove.

3.   Heat the wok over high heat and add 2 tablespoons peanut oil. Then add the black-bean and garlic paste. When the garlic browns, add the marinated beef in a thin layer, moving wok from side to side so meat browns evenly. Turn meat over, brown other side, mixing with paste. After browning, remove meat and set aside.

4.   Stir the prepared sauce well and pour into the wok, stirring continuously until it boils. Then add meat and peppers. Mix thoroughly and serve hot.

NOTE: To make ginger juice: Peel and dice 1 slice of ginger; drop pieces into a garlic press, and press to extract the juice.

	SEUN MOI OP
	Steamed Duck with Preserved Plums

This dish is very much a wedding of opposites, the sweetness of candy and the sourness of plums coming together in harmony.

1 duck, 4½ pounds

Stuffing ingredients:
  9 preserved plums, after pitting about 2½
        tablespoons
  5 garlic cloves: peel, mash, and mince finely
  2 tablespoons brown bean sauce
  1 teaspoon salt
  ⅓ cup rock candy: mash to fine particles with a
        mallet (or brown sugar)
  1 tablespoon dark soy sauce, to coat duck
  1½ tablespoons peanut oil, to fry duck

1.   Clean the duck thoroughly, removing all the membranes and fat. Wash under running water and dry thoroughly with paper towels. Allow the duck to drain in a strainer over a bowl so that all the water drips off.

2.   Combine stuffing ingredients in a bowl and mix. Coat whole duck with soy sauce, using your fingers. Fill the cavity of the duck with the stuffing. Close openings with skewers.

3.   Heat a wok over high heat, add peanut oil, and use a spatula to coat the sides of the wok with oil. When white smoke appears, sear the duck in the wok. Turn over frequently until whole duck is browned. Remove and let cool.

4.   Place duck, breast side up, in a steaming dish. Steam for 45 to 60 minutes (see steaming directions, page 46).

5.   Preheat oven to 375° to 400° F. for 15 minutes. Roast duck, breast side down, for 10 minutes, then turn over and cook other side for 10 minutes. Reduce temperature 25° to 50°, depending upon whether duck is burning, and roast for another 25 minutes. When duck is a deep golden brown and the skin is crispy, remove and serve.

NOTE: The roasting step is to suit American tastes. In Hong Kong, the duck would be steamed until tender, and served. Classically, this is a steamed duck, but I have found that most Americans prefer to have duck roasted.

SZE GUA TONG

Silk Squash Soup with Shredded Pork

The silk squash is an odd vegetable, shaped like a cucumber but with ridges along its length, ridges that must be pared off before the squash is prepared. It was a special treat for me as a girl in China because it was available only from late spring to early summer, less than two months a year. It is available at all times here. Select small, young silk squashes because they are very sweet.

3 pounds silk squash
12 ounces lean fresh pork (pork butt)

For marinade, combine in a bowl and mix well:
   1 teaspoon light soy sauce
   2 teaspoons oyster sauce
   1 teaspoon sesame oil
   ½ teaspoon whiskey, Shwo-Hsing wine, or sherry
 1½ teaspoons salt
 1½ teaspoons sugar
   2 teaspoons cornstarch
    Pinch of white pepper

  2 tablespoons lard or peanut oil
1½ teaspoons salt
  1 slice of ginger, ½ inch thick
8½ cups cold water
 ½ teaspoon baking soda

1. Clean and wash squash, but do not remove all the green. Roll-cut squash: Starting at one end, cut diagonally into approximately ¾-inch slices. Turn squash one quarter turn between each cut. Set aside.

2. Shred pork finely. Mix with marinade. Set aside.

3. Heat a wok over high heat; add lard or peanut oil. When a wisp of white smoke appears, add salt and ginger. When ginger browns, add squash and stir-fry until squash turns bright green. Remove squash and place in a large pot.

4. Add cold water and baking soda to the pot and bring to a boil over high heat, uncovered. Lower heat and cook for 3 to 4 minutes, or until squash softens.

5. Raise heat and add pork mixture. Separate, bring back to a boil, then cook over high heat for 2 minutes, and serve.

NOTE: Baking soda preserves the bright green color of the squash.

檸檬蒸鷄

LING MUNG GAI

Lemon Chicken

This is the recipe of my aunt number six. It differs from virtually every other so-called lemon chicken recipe in that there is no frying, no batter, and thus no heaviness at all. It is light and fresh and takes advantage of the fresh lemons with which it is made.

1 whole chicken, 3 pounds
8 ounces chicken cutlets

Ingredients for marinade:
1¼ fresh lemons (5 quarters), thin-skinned lemons
       preferred
  1 tablespoon white wine mixed with 1 teaspoon
       ginger juice
1½ tablespoons light soy sauce
  1 tablespoon oyster sauce
  2 teaspoons sesame oil
  1 tablespoon peanut oil
  2 teaspoons salt
  2 teaspoons sugar
  ⅛ teaspoon white pepper
  3 to 3½ tablespoons cornstarch

15 sprigs of coriander or parsley

1.   Chop chicken and chicken cutlet into bite-size pieces and rinse thoroughly and individually, to ensure that there will be no small pieces or chips of bone. Drain off excess water, dry chicken pieces with paper towel, and place in a very large mixing bowl.

2.   Squeeze 5 lemon quarters over the chicken and place 4 quarters in with the chicken pieces. Add remaining marinade ingredients. When all ingredients have been added to chicken, the entire mixture should be hand-tossed. Let the chicken and marinade stand for at least 1 hour.

3. Place chicken in a steamproof dish or cake pan and spread the pieces as much as possible. Pour remainder of marinade into the dish as well (see steaming directions, page 46).

4. Steam the chicken from 30 to 50 minutes, turning chicken 2 or 3 times during cooking. The steaming process is complete when the chicken turns white.

5. Remove chicken from wok and place in a serving dish. Garnish with about 15 sprigs of coriander or parsley. Serve immediately.

NOTE: If chicken has too much liquid, add 1 teaspoon cornstarch mixed with 1 teaspoon cold water and stir constantly until blended. If cornstarch is added, increase steaming time by 5 minutes.

During the steaming process keep additional boiling water at hand to replenish water in pot or wok.

❧ *This recipe can be prepared 1 to 2 days in advance. Chicken can be reheated in a pot over low heat; stir frequently.*

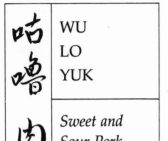

WU
LO
YUK

*Sweet and
Sour Pork*

The origins of this popular dish lie somewhat north of
Canton, somewhat south of Peking. It is one of those
preparations that is virtually universal in China, and just
about everywhere else, but in the course of time it has
come to be thought of as Cantonese. It is certainly true
that the Cantonese prepare it better than anyone else. In
fact, when Prince Philip, the Duke of Edinburgh, visited
Hong Kong, it was the first food he asked for.

½ cup fresh sweet red pepper
½ cup fresh green pepper
½ cup pineapple
¼ cup carrots
12 ounces pork, fresh ham or pork butt, cut into 1-inch
     cubes
2 tablespoons cornstarch

For batter, combine in a bowl:
¾ cup flour
¾ cup cornstarch
½ teaspoon salt
1 tablespoon baking powder
9 ounces cold water
1½ tablespoons peanut oil

To make a sauce, combine and mix in a pot:
9 tablespoons red-wine vinegar
9 tablespoons sugar
6 tablespoons tomato sauce
2¼ tablespoons cornstarch mixed with 2¼
     tablespoons cold water
2½ teaspoons dark soy sauce
¾ cup cold water

1.   Wash peppers, dry thoroughly, and cut into ¾-inch
cubes. Cut pineapple into ¾-inch cubes. Cut carrots into
slices ¾ by ¼ inch. Coat cubes of meat with cornstarch and
set aside.

2. Make the batter: Place flour, cornstarch, salt, and baking powder in a bowl. Pour in cold water gradually, stirring clockwise with chopsticks until mixture is smooth. Add peanut oil; mix. Set aside.

3. Stir sauce ingredients together over medium heat, stirring constantly, until boiling. Add vegetables and pineapple. Bring back to a boil. Sauce is done. Turn heat off. Set aside.

4. For deep-frying: Heat a wok, add peanut oil, and heat until a wisp of white smoke can be seen. Holding pork cubes with chopsticks, dip into batter and place gently in oil. Cook for 30 seconds, turn over; cook until golden brown, turning often, about 5 minutes. Drain the meat and place in a heatproof dish, which has been preheated.

5. Reheat sauce, stirring constantly, for 1 to 2 minutes, until very hot. Pour into a sauceboat; serve with pork and with cooked rice.

NOTE: This can be prepared ahead, early on the day it is to be served. Follow all meat instructions, but cook until three quarters cooked, only light brown. Drain and reserve. Before serving, place in hot oil for 2 minutes. The sauce, however, *must* be made just before serving.

SING
JAU
CHAU
MAI
FUN

*Singapore
Noodles*

A preparation that made its way from the Malay Peninsula up the China coast and was cheerfully adopted by the Cantonese.

3 quarts cold water
1 tablespoon salt
6 ounces dry rice noodles
6 ounces chicken cutlet, shredded

For chicken marinade, combine in a bowl and mix well:
½ teaspoon sesame oil
1 teaspoon light soy sauce
1 teaspoon oyster sauce
½ teaspoon ginger juice mixed with ½ teaspoon white wine
½ teaspoon salt
1 teaspoon sugar
¾ teaspoon cornstarch
Pinch of white pepper

½ cup celery
⅓ cup carrots
2 fresh water chestnuts, peeled
½ cup small green peppers
¼ cup bamboo shoots
3 scallions, both ends discarded
5 tablespoons lard or peanut oil
2 garlic cloves, minced

For curry mixture:
1½ tablespoons curry powder mixed with 1½ tablespoons cold water
2½ tablespoons cold water
1 beef bouillon cube
1 slice fresh ginger, ⅛ inch thick

1.   Cook noodles at least 2½ hours before assembling dish. Pour cold water into a large pot, add salt, and bring to a boil. Add noodles and boil for 1 to 2 minutes. Stir while cooking. Cook *al dente.* Remove and rinse twice by filling pot with cold water. Drain well.

2.   Shred chicken; add to marinade; set aside and allow to marinate 30 minutes. Wash and dry vegetables and shred into 2-inch lengths. Set aside.

3.   Make the curry mixture: In a saucepan heat 1 tablespoon lard over high heat. Add 1 minced garlic clove; stir. When garlic browns, add curry powder mixed with 1½ tablespoons cold water. Stir together and let cook for 2 minutes. Add 2½ tablespoons cold water; mix well. Add bouillon cube. Lower heat, cover, and cook for 10 to 15 minutes, stirring 3 to 4 times, until smoothly blended. Set aside.

4.   Heat a wok over high heat; add 1 tablespoon lard or peanut oil and ginger. Add vegetables. Stir-fry for 2 to 3 minutes, until vegetables turn bright colors. Remove from wok and drain well. Remove wok from stove and clean. Replace on stove.

5.   Heat the wok over high heat; add 1 tablespoon lard or peanut oil. When a wisp of white smoke appears, add 1 garlic clove. When garlic turns brown, add sliced chicken. Stir-fry until chicken turns white. Add curry sauce and stir. Remove from wok. Clean wok and replace on stove.

6.   Heat the wok over high heat and add 2 tablespoons lard or peanut oil; coat the wok. When white smoke appears, add noodles. Place rice noodles in wok by allowing them to slide over spatula into wok, thereby avoiding having noodles splatter in the hot oil. Use chopsticks and spatula to toss noodles and to loosen them. If noodles start to burn, lower heat. Cook for 10 minutes; add chicken and combine well with noodles. Add vegetables to mixture and stir well. When combined, turn off heat, remove from wok, place in a platter, and serve immediately.

JING
SEK
BON

*Steamed
Sea Bass*

Steaming fish is very much a southern China, Cantonese technique, and it is a special dish offered at a meal to an honored guest. My husband recalls that when we were courting he was "honored" by my aunt with a good bit of a steamed bass, including its eye.

2 to 2½ pounds whole sea bass (Flounder, striped bass, or red snapper can be substituted.)

Coating ingredients:
2 tablespoons peanut oil
1½ teaspoons sesame oil
2 tablespoons light soy sauce
1 tablespoon white wine
1 to 1½ teaspoons salt
4 slices of fresh ginger, shredded

4 Chinese dried black mushrooms: soak, wash, discard stems, slice finely
4 ounces fresh pork, finely shredded
½ teaspoon sesame oil
2 tablespoons boiled peanut oil
3 scallions: wash, dry, discard both ends, slice finely
1 tablespoon finely chopped fresh coriander (optional)

1.   Clean fish thoroughly, remove intestines and extra fat, and wash inside and out. Dry well and place in a steamproof dish. Mix coating ingredients in a small bowl and sprinkle on inside and outside of fish.

2.   Sprinkle sliced mushrooms over fish. Mix shredded pork with sesame oil and sprinkle that mixture over fish. Let stand for 10 minutes. Place the fish in its dish in a steamer. (If fish is too large it may be cut into halves, though naturally and aesthetically it should remain whole.)

3. See steaming directions, page 46. Steam for 30 to 45 minutes, until a chopstick can be easily inserted into the fish flesh. (If flounder is used, cut time in half.)

4. Remove fish from wok and pour boiled peanut oil on top. It need not be hot when poured over fish. Sprinkle sliced scallions over fish and serve immediately. Garnish with coriander.

NOTE: Boiled peanut oil removes the fish smell from the dish and adds a nice aroma. To prepare the oil, heat it in a wok until wisps of white smoke can be seen, then remove. Boiled peanut oil may be prepared in advance. If kept in a closed jar, it will last for 2 to 3 weeks.

A BANQUET FROM PEKING

GON CHAU NGAU YUK SEE *Twice-Fried Shredded Beef*

BEIJING OP *Peking Duck*

BOK BANG *Pancakes*

CHAU LOONG HAR *Panfried Lobster*

CHUNG BAU YUNG YUK *Sliced Lamb with Scallions*

SEUN LOT TONG *Hot and Sour Soup*

HOT YEE GAI *Beggar's Chicken*

MUK SEE YUK *Moo Shoo Pork*

SIU CHAU TIENTSIN BOK CHOY *Sitr-Fried Tientsin Cabbage*

KEI LUN YUE *Mythical Fish*

PEKING

Cooking of the North

Peking cooking is the most limited of Chinese regional cuisines in terms of variety, but it more than makes up for its narrow range with its art. Its major indigenous foodstuffs are wheat rather than rice, lamb, shellfish from its rivers, and white leafy vegetables such as cabbage and that variety called Tientsin bok choy (which occasionally is referred to as Peking Cabbage).

From its kitchens have come the Mongolian firepot, mutton and lamb in various ways, ground meats sweetened with brown sugar, sweetened soy, and anise-flavored five-spice powder. Peking chefs make wheat noodles, scramble eggs with sugar, and serve steamed wheat-flour buns and loaves far more than they do boiled rice. They are masters of the thin pancake, the Chinese crêpe that is served with Peking Duck and Moo Shoo Pork. Their cooking is drier than the Cantonese, but they use an abundance of sweets. They even have a soy jam they serve on their steamed breads.

It is in Peking that so-called Mandarin cooking was born. Often mistaken for a school of cooking, cooking in the Mandarin way simply means working with great attention to presentation. A Mandarin dish, prepared for the Imperial Court or in the Peking palace kitchens, was supposed to evoke exclamations of admiration from those who were to eat it. Dishes should show meticulous care, detailed cutting, elaborate arranging. Perhaps little ducks of dough should decorate the rim of a serving platter; perhaps a colored dough goldfish should be sitting in the bowl of your spoon when you pick it up to drink your soup.

Peking also became a center for the cooking of all China because it was the seat of power and government, the center which drew representatives from all over the country. Thus its cuisine expanded.

GON
CHAU
NGAU
YUK
SEE

*Twice-Fried
Shredded Beef*

8 ounces flank steak, shredded

Combine to make a marinade:
1 tablespoon egg white
1½ tablespoons cornstarch
¼ teaspoon whiskey
Pinch of white pepper

Make the sauce in a bowl:
2 teaspoons dark soy sauce
1 tablespoon sugar
2 tablespoons chicken broth
1 teaspoon white vinegar
½ teaspoon sesame oil
½ teaspoon Hunan pepper

3½ cups peanut oil
3 dried chili peppers
1½ teaspoons minced fresh ginger
2 teaspoons minced garlic
¾ cup very finely shredded carrot, 1½-inch lengths
3 scallions: discard both ends, wash, dry, cut into 1½-inch lengths, shred white portions
Sprigs of coriander or parsley for garnish

1. Marinate flank steak in the marinade, refrigerated, for 4 hours. (There will be virtually no residue.) Make the sauce and reserve it.

2. Heat a wok over high heat for 1 minute. Add 3½ cups peanut oil and heat to 350° F. Place flank steak in a Chinese strainer, separating the meat pieces, and lower it gently into the hot oil; this is to prevent spattering. Continue to separate the meat with a spatula as it cooks. Fry it for about 2 minutes, until it is crisp. Remove with the strainer and drain over a bowl.

3. Pour oil from the wok into a bowl. Replace 1½ tablespoons of oil in the wok. Heat wok. Add chili peppers and stir. Add ginger and garlic, stirring after each addition.

Add the carrot and scallions. Stir-fry until scallions turn bright green. Return beef to wok. Stir-fry, mixing thoroughly and keeping beef pieces separate, for about 1½ minutes.

4.   Make a well in the center of the mixture. Stir the sauce and add it. Stir thoroughly and mix well until the sauce thickens. Remove from wok and serve immediately, garnished with sprigs of coriander or parsley.

BEIJING OP

Peking Duck

This classic duck recipe from China's Imperial City is as universal a part of Chinese cuisine as any food preparation can be. In Peking there are several Peking Duck restaurants that serve entire banquets composed of duck, of which Peking Duck is just a part. Elsewhere it is regarded, rightly, as a dish quite elegant and special.

1 duck, 5 pounds, whole, including head, wings, and
    feet (freshly killed duck is preferred)
4 cups boiling water or, alternately,
    3 to 4 quarts boiling water to scald the duck

For the coating:
    3 cups boiling water
    3 tablespoons white vinegar
    3 tablespoons maltose or honey

For the sauce, combine and mix well in a bowl:
    ¼ cup hoisin sauce
    ½ teaspoon sugar
    ½ teaspoon sesame oil
    ½ teaspoon Shao-Hsing wine or sherry

5 scallions: wash, dry, save white portions only; cut
    into 2-inch sections, then cut edges to make
    fringes
10 pancakes (see page 99)

Special tools
1 air pump
2 chopsticks or 7-inch sticks

1.   Prepare the duck: Clean, remove all membrane and fat, and rinse inside and outside with cold running water. Allow water to drain. Tie off the neck of the duck with a piece of string and insert the nozzle of the air pump into the neck opening. Inflate with the pump until the skin separates from the flesh.

(You may alternately use your hands to separate the skin from the flesh, but a small air pump makes this step much easier. Separating the skin from the flesh is absolutely essential for Peking Duck.)

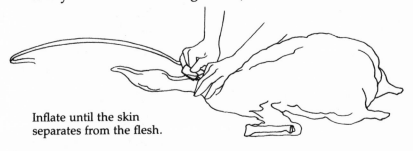

Inflate until the skin
separates from the flesh.

2.   Remove pump nozzle. With a cleaver remove the first 2 joints of each of the duck's wings and feet. Insert a 7-inch stick or chopstick under the wings through the back to lift them away from the body.

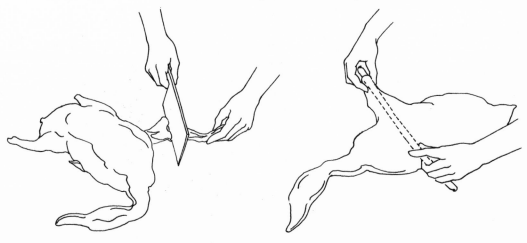

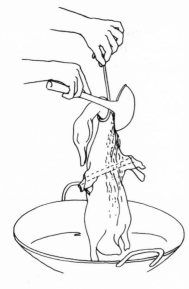

3.   Scalding: Hold the duck with one hand and use the other hand to ladle the boiling water onto the skin of the duck. The entire outside must be scalded. It is advisable to hang the duck on a hook over the sink to ease preparation. The skin will darken and tighten when scalded. Allow 30 minutes for skin to dry; on humid days this may take longer.

(Alternate scalding: Bring 3 to 4 quarts water to a boil. Attach a hook to the string around the duck's neck. Holding the hook, insert the duck into the boiling water.)

4.   Coating: In a wok mix together boiling water, vinegar, and maltose and bring to a boil. Hang the duck either by the neck or under the wings. (Hanging the duck may seem to be a problem, but in fact it is very easy. Attach a string around the duck's neck or under the wings. Hang the string on a hook over a sink, or on a window sill, or between two chairs, supporting a stick between them. Place paper under the duck to catch drippings.) Ladle the coating onto the skin of the duck, making sure skin is thoroughly coated. Allow 10 to 12 hours of drying time. (You may use an electric fan and reduce the process to 4 to 5 hours.)

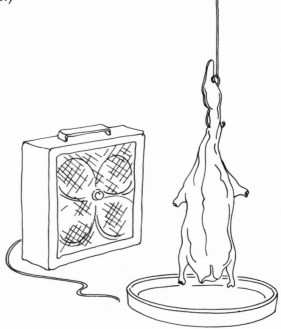

5. To roast: Preheat oven to 450° to 475° F. for 30 minutes. Place a large roasting pan containing at least 1 inch of water on the bottom shelf of the oven, then place duck directly on an oven rack over the roasting pan.

Roast duck breast side down for 10 minutes, then reduce temperature to 425° F. Turn the duck over and allow other side to roast for 10 minutes. If duck is burning, reduce the temperature to 400° F.

Allow duck to cook evenly for another 45 minutes, turning frequently to ensure that head and tail do not burn. The duck is ready when the skin is a deep brown color, and crispy. Remove and allow to cool for 2 to 3 minutes.

6. To serve: First slice the duck skin off in irregular scalloplike pieces. Then slice the meat similarly. Serve the duck wrapped in a pancake that contains 1 teaspoon of hoisin sauce mixture, 1 scallion brush, 2 pieces of meat, and 2 pieces of skin.

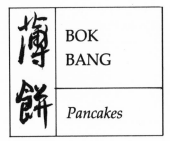

BOK
BANG

Pancakes

1¾ cups high-gluten flour
¾ cup water, brought to a boil
½ cup flour, for dusting
1½ teaspoons sesame oil

1. In a mixing bowl, place the high-gluten flour. Slowly add the boiling water and mix with 2 pairs of chopsticks or a wooden spoon in one direction. When flour absorbs the water and cools, knead the dough into a ball, then place dough on a work surface dusted with flour. Knead for about 2 minutes, until dough is thoroughly mixed. Place in a mixing bowl, cover with plastic wrap, and allow to sit for 30 minutes.

2. On the work surface roll the dough into a 12-inch sausage, then divide into 12 equal pieces. Dust work surface again with flour and flatten each piece with the palm of your hand, using additional flour to dust if the dough is sticky. Cover unused dough with plastic wrap.

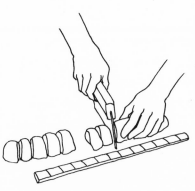

3. Working with 2 pieces at a time, wipe top of one gently with sesame oil and place the other flattened piece on top. Dust with flour if necessary and roll them into circles 7 inches in diameter. The result will be a 2-layer pancake.

4. Heat a wok over low-medium heat for about 1 minute. Put the double pancake in the hot dry wok and cook for 1 minute, until the pancake begins to bubble up. Heat in the dry wok must be carefully controlled. If too high, pancakes will burn. Turn over and cook until a few brown spots are visible. Remove from the wok and separate the 2 layers. You will have 2 pancakes, each browned lightly on one side, white on the other. Repeat until all dough is used.

5. To reheat the pancakes, steam them for 5 to 7 minutes and serve.

❧ *These pancakes can be made ahead of time and frozen for up to 3 months. Allow them to defrost before steaming.*

妙 CHAU
龍 LOONG
蝦 HAR

*Panfried
Lobster*

1 whole 2-pound lobster; fresh lobster is necessary,
   killed but not boiled

**For lobster marinade, combine in a bowl and mix
well:**
1½ teaspoons light soy sauce
  1 tablespoon oyster sauce
  ¾ teaspoon salt
  1 teaspoon sugar
    Pinch of white pepper
  2 teaspoons sesame oil

4 ounces fresh pork

For pork marinade, combine in a bowl and mix well:
  ⅛ teaspoon salt
  ¼ teaspoon light soy sauce
  ¼ teaspoon sesame oil
  ½ teaspoon cornstarch
  ½ teaspoon sugar

4 tablespoons peanut oil
2 garlic cloves, minced
1 egg, beaten
2 teaspoons minced ginger
1 tablespoon white wine
2 scallions: discard both ends, cut into fine slices
   Sprigs of coriander

1.   Cut lobster into bite-size pieces. Place in lobster marinade for 30 minutes. Reserve.

2.   Cut pork into ¼-inch dice. Place in pork marinade for
20 minutes. Reserve.

3.   Heat a wok over high heat for 1 minute. Add 1 tablespoon peanut oil and coat wok with a spatula. Add 1
minced garlic clove. When it browns, add pork mixture,
separating pieces of pork. Let cook for 3 minutes. Turn
over and mix thoroughly.

4.   When pork turns white, add beaten egg, and mix into a soft scramble. Remove from wok and reserve.

5.   Wash and dry wok. Drain lobster; reserve the marinade.

6.   Heat the wok over high heat for 1 minute. Add 3 tablespoons peanut oil; coat wok. Add minced ginger; stir. Add second minced garlic clove. When garlic browns, add lobster pieces.

7.   Spread lobster pieces in a single layer, turning wok side to side to spread heat evenly. Turn over pieces. Add white wine at edges of wok and allow it to run down; mix thoroughly.

8.   When lobster meat reddens, add pork-egg mixture. Mix all ingredients thoroughly. If too dry, add a little of the reserved lobster marinade. Add scallions. Mix thoroughly. Remove from wok, place in a serving dish, and garnish with sprigs of coriander.

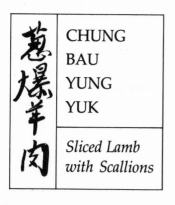

CHUNG
BAU
YUNG
YUK

*Sliced Lamb
with Scallions*

8 ounces of lamb, weighed after trimming. Leg fillet is recommended. Cut into slices 1½ by 2 inches

For marinade for lamb, combine in a bowl and mix well:
  2 teaspoons sesame oil
  1 teaspoon peanut oil
  4 teaspoons dark soy sauce
  1 teaspoon Shao-Hsing wine or sherry
  ½ teaspoon white vinegar
  1 teaspoon sugar
  1½ teaspoons cornstarch
    Pinch of white pepper

2½ tablespoons peanut oil
  8 ounces scallions: discard both ends, wash, dry, cut
        into 1½-inch pieces; quarter thick white portions
  1 tablespoon minced ginger
  1 teaspoon minced garlic
  2 teaspoons Shao-Hsing wine or sherry

For a sauce, combine in a bowl and mix well:
  ¼ teaspoon salt
  ½ teaspoon sugar
  1 teaspoon cornstarch
  ½ teaspoon white vinegar
     Pinch of white pepper
  3 tablespoons chicken broth
  1 teaspoon sesame oil

Sprigs of coriander

1. Marinate lamb for 1 hour. Reserve.

2. Heat a wok over high heat for 1 minute. Add 1 tablespoon peanut oil. Add scallions and stir-fry for 30 seconds. Remove and set aside.

3. Wipe off wok and spatula with dry paper towel. Heat wok again over high heat for 1 minute. Add remaining peanut oil, coating sides of wok with the spatula. Add ginger; stir. Add garlic; stir. When garlic browns add the lamb and marinade.

4. Spread meat in a single layer. Cook for 1 minute. Turn over. Add wine around edges of wok; stir. Add stir-fried scallions and mix well. Make a well in the center of the mixture and add sauce. Mix thoroughly. Turn off heat; add sesame oil. Mix well. Place on serving dish, garnish with coriander sprigs, and serve.

酸
辣
湯

| SEUN |
| LOT |
| TONG |

Hot and Sour
Soup

7 cups chicken broth
1 whole garlic clove
1 slice of fresh ginger, ½ inch thick
2 tablespoons cloud ears: soak in hot water for 30
    minutes, wash, set aside
60 dried tiger lily buds: soak in hot water until soft,
    remove hard ends, cut into halves
4 tablespoons mustard pickle, shredded, or 1 teaspoon
    white pepper
6 slices of dried bean curd: soak in hot water until soft
½ pound fresh pork, shredded

For pork marinade, combine in a bowl and mix well:
⅛ teaspoon salt
¼ teaspoon light soy sauce
1 teaspoon sesame oil
1 teaspoon sugar
½ teaspoon cornstarch

3 to 4 tablespoons red-wine vinegar
6 tablespoons cornstarch mixed with 6 tablespoons
    cold water
3 to 4 eggs, beaten
2 cakes fresh bean curd: cut into strips ¼ inch thick
2 to 3 teaspoons dark soy sauce
1 tablespoon sesame oil
4 tablespoons finely sliced scallions

1.   Heat chicken broth in a large pot. Add garlic and ginger. Cover pot. Bring to a boil and add cloud ears. Cover and cook for 5 minutes. Lower heat.

2.   Add tiger lily buds; cook for another minute, covered. Add mustard pickle (or pepper) and dried bean curd and cook for another 2 minutes. Each time an ingredient is added, the pot must be covered again.

3. Raise heat and add pork and marinade; bring to a boil. Add the vinegar and stir. Stir cornstarch mixture. Using a ladle, stir soup continuously in one direction. Slowly pour in cornstarch mixture. Continue stirring until cornstarch thickens. Add beaten eggs in the same manner. If soup is too thick, thin with additional chicken broth.

4. Add fresh bean curd; stir again. Add soy sauce and sesame oil; stir. Turn off heat. Serve immediately, sprinkling each individual bowl of soup with sliced scallion.

NOTE: Dried bean curd can be kept indefinitely in a jar in a dry place. Fresh bean curd can be kept for 2 to 3 weeks if refrigerated, and if the water they are stored in is changed daily.

HOT YEE GAI
Beggar's Chicken

This justly famous preparation from Peking derives its name from a folk tale about a beggar, without home, money, or food, who stole a chicken from a farm and raced off with it. To cook it, he covered it with mud, made a fire in a hole in the ground, and baked his chicken, peeling the feathers off before he ate. Some people feel that the chicken is too rich for such a story and call it Foo Guai Gai, or Rich and Noble Chicken, a name which I prefer.

1 whole chicken, 3 to 3¼ pounds: clean, remove fat
    and membranes

For marinade, combine in a bowl and mix well:
    3 tablespoons Ng Ga Pei spirits, or whiskey
    1 cinnamon stick, broken into 4 pieces
    2 pieces of 8-star anise
1¼ teaspoons salt
    Pinch of white pepper
2½ teaspoons sugar

Stuffing ingredients:
1½ cups diced onions
 ½ cup pork fat, cut into ⅛-inch dice
 6 dried black mushrooms: wash, soak until
      softened, discard stems, dice caps into ½-inch
      pieces
 ⅓ cup preserved vegetable: wash 5 to 7 times; open
      leaves and rinse thoroughly, squeeze, slice
      finely
 2 teaspoons Shao-Hsing wine or sherry
 1 teaspoon sesame oil
 ½ teaspoon 5-spice powder
 ½ teaspoon salt
    Pinch of white pepper
 2 teaspoons sugar

1½ tablespoons peanut oil

Dough ingredients:
 4 cups high-gluten flour
1¾ cups hot water
 2 teaspoons peanut oil

Special tools
1 yard cheesecloth
2 feet heavy-duty foil wrap

1. Wash chicken; allow to drain thoroughly. Mix marinade ingredients and hand-rub inside and outside of chicken. Place chicken in a dish and set aside.

2. Prepare the stuffing: Assemble all ingredients as specified. In a wok over high heat place peanut oil; when white smoke appears, add onions and cook until brown. Lower heat to medium and add pork fat; stir-fry until transparent. Add mushrooms and preserved vegetable and mix. Turn heat to high, add wine, and stir all ingredients together. Add sesame oil, 5-spice powder, salt, pepper, and sugar. Remove from heat, place in a bowl, and allow to cool.

3. Prepare the dough: Place the flour on a work surface and make a well in the center. Add the hot water slowly with one hand and mix with the other. When water is absorbed, knead for about 2 minutes, until a dough is formed. Coat your hands with peanut oil and rub the dough with some pressure to coat it. Rub your hands over the work surface as well. Flatten the dough on the surface until it is large enough to wrap the chicken completely.

4. Stuff the chicken, by placing the stuffing loosely in the cavity. Close the neck and tail openings with toothpicks or metal skewers.

5. Wrap the chicken completely in the cheesecloth. Place the wrapped chicken in the center of the flattened dough and wrap the chicken, sealing the edges of the dough by pressing it closed with the fingers. Spread out the foil wrap and place the chicken, breast side up, on it and fold the foil around the chicken, closing it.

6. Preheat oven to 300° to 350° F. for 15 minutes. Place wrapped chicken in a roasting pan and bake for 4 hours. Unwrap and serve slices of chicken and spoonfuls of the stuffing.

NOTE: The covering insulates the chicken so that it will remain hot enough to serve if removed from the oven 1 to 2 hours prior to serving.

木須肉	MUK SEE YUK
	Moo Shoo Pork

How, you might ask, does Muk See Yuk become Moo Shoo Pork? Well, the first version is the way we Cantonese pronounce this lovely dish from Peking. If they want to call it Moo Shoo Pork, that's quite all right.

10 pancakes (see page 99)
3 cups peanut oil
1 cup shredded lean pork
1 teaspoon minced ginger

 1 teaspoon minced garlic

 4 cups finely shredded cabbage

 3 scallions: discard both ends, wash, dry, cut into 1½-inch pieces (quarter thick white portions)

 ½ cup shredded bamboo shoots

 2 tablespoons cloud ears: soak in hot water for 30 minutes, wash, reserve

40 tiger lily buds: soak in hot water for 30 minutes, cut off hard ends, cut across into halves

 5 dried Chinese black mushrooms: soak in hot water for 30 minutes, remove stems, wash, shred

For a sauce, combine in a bowl and mix well:

3½ teaspoons sugar

 ¾ teaspoon salt

1½ teaspoons Shao-Hsing wine or sherry

 2 tablespoons dark soy sauce

 1 tablespoon cornstarch

 2 tablespoons chicken broth

1½ tablespoons hoisin sauce

  Pinch of white pepper

 4 eggs, lightly scrambled

 1 tablespoon sesame oil

1. Make the pancakes.

2. Heat a wok. Add 3 cups peanut oil and heat to 350° F. Add pork and oil-blanch for 2 to 3 minutes, until pork loses its pinkness. Remove meat from oil with a strainer and allow it to drain over a bowl.

3. Empty oil from wok into a bowl; set aside. Return 2 tablespoons oil to wok; heat. Add ginger and garlic; stir for a few seconds. Add cabbage; cook for 3 minutes. Then add scallions, bamboo shoots, cloud ears, tiger lily buds, and mushrooms. Stir, cooking for another 3 minutes.

4. Return pork to the mixture; stir together. Make a well in the center and add the sauce. Mix thoroughly. Add scrambled eggs; stir thoroughly again. Turn off heat, add sesame oil, toss, and serve with the pancakes.

SIU
CHAU
TIENTSIN
BOK
CHOY

*Stir-Fried
Tientsin
Cabbage*

This cabbage, which goes by many names including Peking Cabbage, Shantung Cabbage, even Napa Cabbage, is a versatile vegetable that picks up the tastes of whatever it is combined with. This is the way it is prepared in Peking.

1 pound Tientsin cabbage
2 tablespoons peanut oil
2 teaspoons minced ginger
8 dried Chinese black mushrooms: soak in hot water
    for 30 minutes, wash, dry, discard stems, cut into
    julienne
½ cup winter bamboo shoots, cut into julienne
¼ cup sweet red pepper: wash, dry, remove seeds, cut
    into julienne

To make the sauce, combine in a bowl and mix well:
1½ teaspoons oyster sauce
 1 teaspoon dark soy sauce
 1 teaspoon sugar
½ teaspoon salt
 2 teaspoons cornstarch
½ teaspoon sesame oil
½ teaspoon white vinegar
½ teaspoon Shao-Hsing wine or sherry
 3 tablespoons cold water

1. Separate cabbage into individual leaves. Wash thoroughly; drain off excess water. Separate the ribs from the leaves. Cut the ribs into julienne; thinly slice the leaves. Separate sliced ribs and leaves into piles.

2. Heat a wok over high heat for 1 minute. Add peanut oil; coat the wok with a spatula. Add ginger and stir for 20 seconds. Add ribs of cabbage and mushrooms and stir well. Add bamboo shoots; stir well. Add cabbage leaves, mix well, and cook for 1 minute. Add red pepper, mix thoroughly, and cook for 2 minutes more.

3. Make a well in the center, stir sauce, pour into well, and mix thoroughly until the sauce thickens. Remove from wok and serve immediately.

KEI
LUN
YUE

Mythical Fish

This fish preparation, it is said, was a favorite in the Imperial dining rooms of the Ch'ing dynasty. Its name, Kei Lun, represents an animal with the body of a horse and the head of a dragon, a symbol of great good luck. As a matter of fact, the symbol has been retained to this day. Just look at the label of a bottle of the Japanese beer called Kirin, or Kei Lun.

1 whole sea bass or yellowfish

To make a marinade, combine in a bowl and mix well:
  1 teaspoon white vinegar
1½ tablespoons white wine
1½ tablespoons light soy sauce
  2 tablespoons peanut oil
  1 tablespoon shredded fresh ginger
  1 teaspoon salt
    Pinch of white pepper

  3 slices of Smithfield or Virginia ham
  4 large dried Chinese black mushrooms: soak in hot
      water, wash, discard stems, cut caps into halves
  2 tablespoons scallion oil (see page 24)
  4 scallions: wash, retain only white portions, thread
20 strips of sweet red pepper
10 pieces of coriander

1. Wash fish in cold water; remove all membranes and scales. Dry and drain thoroughly.

2. Score fish by making slices approximately the width of the fish in its sides, about 1 inch apart. Cuts should be made up to the bone and with the blade held at an angle, on both sides of the fish. Place the fish in a cake pan or heatproof dish, add the marinade, and set aside.

3. Slice the ham into rectangular pieces, 3 inches by ½ inch and about ⅛ inch thick. Slip the ham slices and the cut mushroom caps into the scores made in the fish, alternating the ham and the mushrooms.

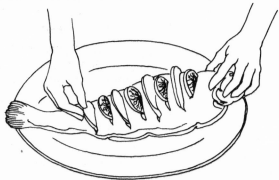

4. Place the fish, which is in the heatproof dish, in the wok and steam for 10 to 12 minutes (see steaming directions on page 46).

5. Remove cover and pour scallion oil on fish. Add scallions, pepper strips, and coriander. Serve immediately.

A BANQUET FROM SHANGHAI

SOI JING HAR KAU	*Crystal Shrimp*
JUNG BAO GAI DING	*Chicken with Hoisin Sauce*
SEUT CHOI CHAU NGAU	*Beef and Pickled Shanghai Cabbage*
MUN JIU YUK	*Pork Stew*
LUNG TONG	*Dragon Soup*
LONG JIN OP	*Tea-Smoked Duck*
NGA CHOI SAH LUT	*Shanghai Bean-Sprout Salad*
LEUNG MEIN WONG	*Panfried Noodles*
WOO JOOK BAU YUE	*Shanghai Fish Rolled in Bean Curd*

SHANGHAI
Cooking of the East

The cooks of Shanghai will tell you, without the least trace of modesty, that to eat the best Cantonese food you should travel to Shanghai. Predictably, they say the same thing about Peking and Szechuan cooking. With good reason. The cooking in Shanghai is certainly the most cosmopolitan in China, as befits the country's most cosmopolitan city, and its cooks as a group are most accomplished and versatile. I suspect more than a few of them come originally from my hometown of Sun Tak, of which it is said in China, "If you were born in Sun Tak, then you were born to cook." Whatever the reasons, the food they produce tends to be a distillation of all that is best of China's cooking as a whole.

This is not to say that there is not a distinctive Shanghai cuisine; there is. Their food is heavier, a bit sweeter, more oily than that of Canton. It relies heavily on seafood from the streams and canals and lakes of eastern China, in cities such as Hangzhou or Suzhou, which contribute to the Shanghai-eastern kitchen. Hangzhou is the home of Long Jin (Dragon Well) tea, which is used to smoke foods; Suzhou is where it is said the finest food carvers work.

Shanghai people eat more noodles than do people in Canton, though not as much as do the citizens of Peking.

Nor are the noodles steamed. In Shanghai they panfry them, adding vegetables to them. The Shanghai cooks preserve many vegetables, smoke foods, use white vinegars, and often "red-cook" or stew their meat dishes. Even their dim sum, specialties such as the so-called pot sticker dumplings and others filled with soup, are of heavier doughs than those favored by the Cantonese. They mix many foods together occasionally—two kinds of meat, with perhaps shrimp or scallops, and vegetables—and flavor them with honey or sugar, or even the sherrylike Shao-Hsing wine that is made in Shanghai and exported throughout China.

Shanghai cooks are concerned with the appearance of what they cook, so sauces should make the foods they cover shiny with glaze; platters of cold appetizers should be phoenixes, dragons, pheasants, and peacocks; shrimp should glisten. Most often they do.

水晶蝦球	SOI JING HAR KAU
	Crystal Shrimp

This elegant dish is famous in Shanghai, and the name is descriptive of its appearance. The shrimp, after cooking, have almost a crystalline, translucent glaze, and are as beautiful to look at as they are delicious to eat.

20 medium shrimp: shell, devein, wash, dry
  1 egg white, beaten
 ½ teaspoon salt
   Pinch of white pepper
  1 teaspoon white wine
1½ teaspoons cornstarch

To make a sauce, combine in a bowl:
  4 tablespoons sugar
  4 tablespoons white vinegar
  5 tablespoons chicken broth
  4 tablespoons white wine
 ½ teaspoon light soy sauce
 ¼ teaspoon salt
   Pinch of white pepper
  1 teaspoon cornstarch
   White portion of 1 scallion, thinly sliced
  1 thin slice of fresh ginger, cut into 6 pieces

3½ cups peanut oil
  1 tablespoon shredded ginger
1½ tablespoons shredded sweet red pepper
  1 tablespoon shredded scallions
   Sprigs of coriander

1. Marinate shrimp in egg white, salt, pepper, wine, and cornstarch for 1 hour. Combine all sauce ingredients; set aside.

2. Heat a wok over high heat for 40 seconds; add peanut oil. When a wisp of white smoke appears, add shrimp and oil-blanch them until they become pink and curl up. Remove shrimp from wok with a strainer and drain over a bowl.

3. Pour oil from wok. Place wok back over high heat for 40 seconds, or until residue of oil is hot. Add ginger, red pepper, and scallions and stir-fry for 30 seconds to 1 minute. Add shrimp and mix thoroughly.

4. Stir, add sauce, and mix all ingredients together until shrimp are coated. Remove shrimp from wok, place in serving dish, garnish them with coriander, and serve.

JUNG
BAO
GAI
DING

*Chicken with
Hoisin Sauce*

The people of Shanghai tell a story about this dish. It seems the crown prince was traveling incognito about China and came upon a small restaurant in Shanghai, where it was fed to him. He is reported to have interrupted his trip and returned to Peking in order to tell the Imperial chef about it. It is a lovely story about a lovely preparation.

1 pound chicken cutlets, diced into ½-inch pieces

For marinade, combine in a bowl and mix well:
 ½ teaspoon salt
 1 teaspoon sugar
 1 teaspoon light soy sauce
 2 teaspoons white wine mixed with 1 teaspoon
    ginger juice
 1 tablespoon oyster sauce
 1 teaspoon sesame oil
 3 teaspoons cornstarch
   Pinch of white pepper

4½ tablespoons peanut oil
¼ teaspoon salt
1 slice fresh ginger
¾ cup green snap beans: wash, dry, remove ends, cut
       into ½-inch pieces
¼ cup fresh water chestnuts: dice into ¼-inch pieces
½ cup bamboo shoots: dice into ¼-inch pieces
¾ cup sweet red pepper: dice into ½-inch pieces
2 garlic cloves, minced
2 tablespoons hoisin sauce
1½ tablespoons white wine
½ cup raw cashews: dry-roast over very low heat until
       lightly browned, then set aside

1. Cover chicken with marinade and let it marinate for 30 minutes.

2. Heat 1½ tablespoons peanut oil over high heat with salt and ginger until ginger browns. Add vegetables in this order: green beans, water chestnuts, bamboo shoots, peppers; stir as they are added. Cook for 1 minute, then remove from wok with a strainer. Drain; reserve. Wash wok.

3. Heat remaining oil over high heat with minced garlic until garlic browns. Add hoisin sauce and mix well. Add marinated chicken in a thin layer, cook for 30 seconds, then turn over.

4. Add white wine around edge of wok so that it trickles into the chicken mixture. When chicken turns white, add vegetables and stir together.

5. Remove from heat and serve. Place roasted cashews to the side to be added in whatever quantity the diner sees fit. The reason for this is that the nuts, if mixed with the chicken and vegetables, tend to soften and become soggy.

NOTE: Cashews may be roasted in advance. Allow to cool and keep in a covered jar before using.

SEUT
CHOI
CHAU
NGAU

*Beef and
Pickled
Shanghai
Cabbage*

This is a traditional dish in Shanghai, noteworthy because the vegetable with which it is prepared, Seut Choy, or Shanghai Cabbage, a leafy stalked vegetable, is never eaten freshly picked. It is raised to be preserved. People in Shanghai salt it for several days, then pack it in jars to be cooked with meats and fish. It is widely available in small cans; after opening, the cabbage can be kept in a sealed jar, refrigerated, almost indefinitely.

12 ounces "oyster cut" London broil: slice into thin
     pieces ½ inch by 2½ inches

For a marinade, combine in a bowl:
  1 tablespoon beaten egg white
  1 teaspoon Shao-Hsing wine or sherry
  1 teaspoon white vinegar
 ¼ teaspoon salt
2½ teaspoons cornstarch
 ½ teaspoon sugar

3 tablespoons ¼-inch pieces of Shanghai Cabbage
½ cup bamboo shoots, cut into julienne
½ cup white portions of scallions, cut into julienne
3 large water chestnuts: peel, wash, dry, cut into
    julienne

For a sauce, combine in a bowl:
  1 teaspoon Shao-Hsing wine or sherry
  1 teaspoon white vinegar
 ⅛ teaspoon salt
1¼ teaspoons sugar
1½ teaspoons dark soy sauce
  1 teaspoon sesame oil
1½ teaspoons cornstarch
    Pinch of white pepper
 ½ cup chicken broth

 5 cups peanut oil
 2 teaspoons minced ginger
1½ teaspoons minced garlic
   Sprigs of coriander

1.   Mix meat with marinade by hand. Refrigerate for 2 hours. Place all prepared vegetables in a dish and reserve. Make sauce and reserve.

2.   Heat a wok over high heat for 1 minute. Add peanut oil and heat to 325° to 350° F. Place meat in a Chinese strainer and lower into oil. Spread meat with spatula; cook for 1½ minutes. Remove meat with a strainer, drain over a bowl, and reserve.

3.   Pour oil from wok into a bowl. Replace 2 tablespoons oil in the wok. Over high heat add ginger and garlic; stir. When garlic browns, add all vegetables and stir well for 1 minute. Add beef and stir thoroughly for 2 more minutes.

4.   Make a well in the center. Stir sauce, pour into well, mix thoroughly. When sauce thickens, it is done. Remove from wok, place in serving dish, garnish with coriander, and serve.

MUN

JIU

YUK

Pork Stew

The reaction from my students to this preparation is usually, "Is this Chinese?" and "Do they really have shallots in China?" The answers are yes and yes. It is very Chinese, traditionally a dish in Shanghai banquets, and favored because it can be prepared in advance. In Shanghai it is also made with pork spareribs.

1½ pounds fresh pork butt or shoulder, with most but not all of fat trimmed
  2 tablespoons cornstarch
  4 to 5 cups peanut oil
  1 slice of ginger
  1 garlic clove, whole
  ¼ cup diced shallots
  1 garlic clove, minced

> **For a sauce, combine in a bowl and mix well:**
>   1 teaspoon sesame oil
>   2 teaspoons light soy sauce
> 1½ tablespoons catsup
> 1¼ teaspoons salt
> 1½ teaspoons sugar
> 1½ tablespoons oyster sauce
>   Pinch of white pepper

1½ tablespoons white wine
  ½ cup chicken broth
  1 large green bell pepper, cut into 1½-inch cubes
  1 large red bell pepper, cut into 1½-inch cubes

1.   Cut fresh pork into 1½-inch cubes. Coat with cornstarch. Spread pork in a single layer in a strainer.

2.   Heat peanut oil in a wok to 375° to 400° F. Add the slice of ginger and the whole garlic clove. When garlic browns, add pork in the strainer. Oil-blanch the coated pork in the hot oil for 2 minutes. Remove, allow to drain over a bowl, and reserve.

3. Pour oil from wok, then return 2 tablespoons to wok and turn on high heat. Add shallots and stir for 2 minutes; add minced garlic. When garlic browns, add pork; stir for about 1½ minutes. Add white wine around edge of wok, and mix well.

4. Stir sauce, then add to wok, and combine all ingredients thoroughly, until meat is well coated. Transfer contents of wok to a pot. Add half of the chicken broth to the wok to loosen remaining sauce and add that to pot as well.

5. Over medium heat allow pork stew to come to a boil, then reduce heat, stir, cover pot, and allow to simmer for 1 to 1½ hours, until pork is tender. If sauce is too thick, add some of remaining chicken broth and stir. Occasionally stir so pork does not stick to pot.

6. When pork is tender, turn heat up high, add cubed peppers, and stir in well. When stew comes again to a boil, turn off heat. Serve immediately.

NOTE: This stew can be prepared ahead, but peppers must be added just before serving. The stew can also be frozen for later use, but again, the peppers should be added after it has been reheated.

| LUNG TONG |
| Dragon Soup |

This soup is symbolism in a pot. To many Chinese the lobster is a symbol of the dragon, which is itself an Imperial symbol. So this is an emperor's soup, a rich soup with both lobster and crab meat in it, a dragon soup, and it would not be complete without the dragon's whiskers, which are of course the bean threads.

12 ounces chicken cutlets: remove membranes and fat, cut into ½-inch cubes, about 1½ cups net
2 lobster tails, about 1 pound: shell, devein, wash, dry, cut into ½-inch cubes

For a marinade for chicken, combine in a bowl and mix well:
   1 teaspoon ginger
   2 teaspoons white wine
   1 teaspoon light soy sauce
   1 teaspoon sesame oil
   1 teaspoon oyster sauce
   1 teaspoon sugar
   ¾ teaspoon salt
   ½ teaspoon white vinegar
      Pinch of white pepper
   2 teaspoons cornstarch

For a marinade for lobster, combine in a bowl and mix well:
1½ teaspoons ginger juice
   1 tablespoon white wine
   1 teaspoon light soy sauce
   ¾ teaspoon salt
   ¾ teaspoon sugar
   1 teaspoon sesame oil
      Pinch of white pepper
   ½ teaspoon white vinegar
   1 teaspoon cornstarch

3 cups peanut oil
1 ounce bean threads (half of a package)
6 cups chicken broth combined with 2 cups cold water
1 tablespoon minced ginger
2 garlic cloves, minced
½ cup fresh mushrooms, cut into ½-inch pieces
½ cup bamboo shoots, cut into ½-inch pieces
¾ cup fresh (or frozen) peas
½ pound crab meat
4 egg whites, beaten
¼ cup finely sliced scallions

1.   Marinate chicken and lobster in their individual marinades for 30 minutes; reserve.

2.   Heat a wok over high heat for 40 seconds. Add peanut oil. When a wisp of white smoke appears, add bean threads. These cook virtually immediately, so have a strainer at the ready and pick them out of the oil in 5 seconds. Drain and reserve.

3.   Pour chicken broth and water into a pot. Add ginger and garlic. Cover and bring to a boil. Add mushrooms and bamboo shoots. Cover, again bring to a boil, and let cook for 2 minutes. Add peas and bring to a boil. Add chicken and marinade to pot, stir, and bring again to a boil.

4.   Boil for about 2 minutes, until chicken turns white. Then add lobster meat and marinade; stir. Add crab meat; stir. Bring again to a boil. Add beaten egg white; mix gently with a ladle to allow egg to blend.

5.   Add bean threads to pot. Add scallions. Mix briefly, turn off heat, pour into a tureen, and serve.

NOTE: This can be made in advance, but only one day in advance. However, reserve the egg whites, bean threads, and scallions, and do not add them until the soup is reheated.

LONG
JING
OP

*Tea-Smoked
Duck*

The important ingredient in this fragrant and delicious preparation is Dragon Well Tea, that green tea from Hang-zhou, near Shanghai, which is also called Lung Ching, or in Canton Loong Tsing. When you shop for it you will see it spelled all three ways. It is the same tea, however, and wonderful it is.

1 duck, 5 pounds, whole, freshly killed preferred: wash, clean cavity with running water, remove membrane and fat, and drain

For steaming, combine in a dish:

3 small cinnamon sticks
3 pieces of 8-star anise
3 slices of fresh ginger
2 teaspoons sugar
2 teaspoons salt
⅓ cup white wine

⅔ cup Long Jing tea leaves
6 cups peanut oil
2 dozen dried shrimp chips
2 large tomatoes, sliced

1. Steam the duck: Place duck in a large dish with steaming ingredients. Heat 4 cups water in a wok to boiling and place dish with duck on chopsticks wedged above boiling water. Cover wok. Steam for 1¼ to 1½ hours. During the process check the water in the wok; if it evaporates, replace with boiling water at hand. Following steaming, allow duck to cool.

2. Smoke the duck: Place tea leaves in a dry wok; roast until smoking. Place duck on a rack over the leaves and cover with wok cover. Place a wet cloth around cover where it meets the wok, so no air will be able to enter. Allow duck to smoke for 7 to 10 minutes.

3. Remove duck and roast in an oven heated to 325° to 350° F. until fat has drained off, or about 1 hour. Halfway through, turn duck over. This step is for those who prefer an extra crisp, dry duck. The duck can be deep-fried directly instead.

4.   Deep-fry the duck: Heat the wok over high heat for 1 minute. Add peanut oil and heat to 375° to 400° F. Lower duck into oil with the Chinese strainer. Fry for about 5 minutes. Turn over and fry for another 5 minutes, or until duck is nicely browned. (The duck can be fried in halves if you wish.) Remove, cut duck into bite-size pieces, place on a platter, and surround with shrimp chips and sliced tomatoes.

NOTE: The shrimp chips can be fried in 4 cups peanut oil in advance of the duck, or they can be fried even a day earlier. However, if done in advance they should be kept in a sealed container.

芽菜色拉	NGA CHOI SAH LUT
	Shanghai Bean-Sprout Salad

1½ pounds bean sprouts
  1 medium-size sweet red pepper, thinly sliced
  4 to 5 scallions: discard both ends, cut into 1½-inch
       sections; quarter white portions lengthwise
1½ tablespoons peanut oil
  3 tablespoons white vinegar
1½ to 2 tablespoons sugar
  ½ to 1 tablespoon salt
  1 teaspoon sesame oil

1.   Wash and drain bean sprouts thoroughly. Slice peppers and scallions.

2.   Heat a wok over high heat for 1 minute. Add peanut oil; coat sides of wok with oil, using spatula. When a wisp of white smoke appears, add bean sprouts. Stir-fry for 30 to 45 seconds. Add pepper; stir. Add scallions; stir well. Remove vegetables and place in a strainer; allow liquid to drain off.

3.   Place vegetables in a large mixing bowl. Add vinegar, sugar, salt, and sesame oil; mix well. Refrigerate. Allow to sit overnight before serving.

LEUNG
MEIN
WONG

Panfried
Noodles

8 cups water
8 ounces fresh egg noodles (soft noodles, slightly
        thicker than vermicelli)
5 ounces lean fresh pork, cut into julienne

**For marinade for the pork, combine in a bowl and
mix well:**
  1 teaspoon sesame oil
  ½ teaspoon sugar
  ½ teaspoon salt
  ½ teaspoon white vinegar
  ½ teaspoon Shao-Hsing wine or sherry
  ½ teaspoon cornstarch
  ¼ teaspoon light soy sauce
     Pinch of white pepper

For a sauce, combine in a bowl and mix well:
  2 teaspoons dark soy sauce
  1 teaspoon sugar
  1 teaspoon sesame oil
  1 teaspoon white vinegar
  ½ teaspoon Shao-Hsing wine or sherry
     Pinch of white pepper
  1½ teaspoons cornstarch
  ½ cup chicken broth

  6 to 7 tablespoons peanut oil
  1 slice of fresh ginger, minced
  1 garlic clove, minced
  ½ cup snow peas: remove strings and ends, wash, dry,
        cut into julienne diagonally
  3 fresh water chestnuts: peel, wash, cut into julienne
  ¼ cup bamboo shoots: cut into julienne
  2 scallions: discard both ends, wash, dry, cut into
        julienne

1. Boil water. Add noodles and cook for 1 minute, until *al dente*. Run cold water into the pot and drain noodles in a strainer. Place noodles back in pot, add cold water, drain again. Repeat once again. Allow noodles to drain for 2 hours, turning them occasionally so they are completely dry.

2. Marinate pork for 1 hour; reserve. Make the sauce; reserve.

3. Pour 4 tablespoons peanut oil into a cast-iron frying pan over high heat. Heat for 40 seconds. When a wisp of white smoke appears, place noodles in an even layer in the pan, covering entire pan. Cook for 2 minutes, moving pan about on the burner to ensure noodles brown evenly. Invert noodles using dish placed over fry pan. Cook the other side for 2 minutes. If a bit more oil is needed at this point, pour 1 additional tablespoon oil into pan, but *only* if it is necessary.

4. As noodles are cooking, heat a wok over high heat for 40 seconds. Add 2 tablespoons peanut oil and coat the wok. Add ginger; stir. Add garlic; stir. When garlic browns, add pork and marinade, spread in a thin layer, and cook for 2 minutes. Turn over and mix well.

5. Add all vegetables; stir together. When vegetables have softened slightly, make a well in the center and add sauce. Stir together. When sauce thickens, turn off heat.

6. Place noodles in a dish, pour contents of wok on top, and serve.

WOO
JOOK
BAU YUE

*Shanghai Fish
Rolled
in Bean Curd*

12 ounces fish fillet: sea bass, flounder, or sole

For marinade, combine in a bowl and mix well:
  1 tablespoon white vinegar
  1 tablespoon white wine
1½ teaspoons light soy sauce
  ¾ teaspoon sugar
  1 teaspoon shredded fresh ginger
    Pinch of white pepper
  1 teaspoon sesame oil
  ¼ teaspoon salt

2 tablespoons cornstarch
3 slices of dried bean curd sheets, cut into pieces 6
    inches square
4 to 5 cups peanut oil

1.　Cut fillet into 3 equal portions. Soak in marinade for 10 minutes. Remove from marinade, then dust with cornstarch, and wrap in bean curd.

2.　Heat a wok over high heat for 1 minute. Add peanut oil and heat to 350° F. Holding each bundle with a pair of chopsticks or tongs, lower into oil. Continue to hold with chopsticks until bean curd seals. The fish is ready when the bean curd turns golden brown. Remove, cut into portions, and serve immediately.

SZECHUAN and HUNAN

西方蜀湘菜

Cooking of the West

Generally most people believe Szechuan cooking to be totally, searing hot. It is not. There are hot dishes in Szechuan, to be sure, most of them flavored with or touched by the chili peppers grown in China's largest province, but the Szechuanese will suggest that they eat these chilies, not because they like the heat, but because the chilies stimulate their palates and prepare them for more subtle dishes. As a matter of fact, a Szechuan banquet will have few, if any, hot dishes. I have included several so that our Szechuan banquet becomes a quintessential Szechuan menu containing both the hot and the non-hot.

Hunan food, on the other hand, is exceedingly hot. Though it is believed that the food of Hunan comprises a school of Chinese cuisine all its own, that is not so. Hunanese cooking is quite like that of Szechuan, its neighbor, except that in Hunan there is greater use of preserved foods and heavy oils and fats such as those rendered from pork and chicken. It has become fashionable to differentiate between Szechuan and Hunan cooking these days, but in reality they are, to the Chinese, the cooking of the west.

In Szechuan and Hunan both rice and wheat are grown, and both are eaten, the rice boiled, the wheat made into noodles. Pigs and poultry abound in this land-locked region, as does lamb, particularly in Hunan, and surprisingly beef. Beef has proliferated because of the use of oxen in the region's salt mines, and they have become a source of food as well as a working animal. There are many vegetables in the area as well, not in the abundance that there is in Canton, but enough to complement the many meat dishes, which in the case of Szechuan are roasted, simmered, and oil-blanched. Both the Szechuan-ese and Hunanese sear their meats in oil, later stir-frying them with other ingredients. This makes for a heavier cui-sine in the west.

They use a good bit of salt, to flavor and to preserve. They pickle vegetables. When they cook they like to com-bine flavors so that a dish will have, simultaneously, sweetness and acidity, blandness and aroma. Despite be-ing away from the sea, there is a goodly amount of sea-food, particularly shrimp and other freshwater shellfish. The fish they are fond of is carp, a freshwater fish. Carp is often difficult to find in markets and tends to be quite bony, so I have substituted sea bass for carp in my western recipes because, though it is less sweet than carp, it is rela-tively free of small bones.

A BANQUET FROM SZECHUAN

JI MAH MEIN   *Cold Sesame Noodles*

JI JIU HAR YUN   *Spider Shrimp*

GORN SIU LOONG HAR   *Spicy Lobster*

SEI CHUN CHAU NGAU YUK   *Szechuan Beef*

TUNG GUA YUNG   *Velvet Wintermelon Soup*

HEUNG SO GAI   *Perfumed Chicken*

BOK CHIT YUK   *White Cut Pork*

SEI GUAI DAU   *Four-Season Beans*

SEI CHUN JIN YUE   *Szechuan Panfried Fish*

JI
MAH
MEIN

Cold Sesame Noodles

8 cups water
8 ounces fresh egg noodles, slightly thicker than
    vermicelli
1½ tablespoons sesame oil

To make the Sesame Sauce, combine in a bowl and mix well:
    1 teaspoon sesame-seed paste
    3 tablespoons peanut butter
    2 teaspoons white vinegar
    2 tablespoons mushroom soy sauce
    1¼ teaspoons Hunan pepper sauce
    1 tablespoon sugar
    5 tablespoons chicken broth
        Pinch of white pepper
    2 tablespoons finely sliced scallions
    2 sprigs coriander, broken into pieces

1.   Bring water to a boil. Add noodles and stir. Cook for 1½ minutes, until *al dente*. Run cold water into pot, then drain noodles. Run cold water again into pot and drain noodles. Repeat once again.

2.   Place drained noodles in a mixing bowl and toss with sesame oil. Refrigerate, uncovered, for 1 hour. Meanwhile make Sesame Sauce.

3.   When noodles are cool, toss with Sesame Sauce, place in a serving dish, garnish with coriander, and serve.

JI
JIU
HAR
YUN

Spider Shrimp

To those who fancy stories with their food, some Chinese will suggest that these delicate shrimp lying on a bed of watercress resemble tiny spiders in their webs, thus the name. I'm not sure that I subscribe to that tale, but it *is* imaginative so I pass it along.

12 ounces medium shrimp: shell, devein, wash
    2 bunches of watercress
    4 ounces pork, cut into julienne

For a pork marinade, combine in a bowl and mix well:
¼ egg white, beaten
¼ teaspoon salt
½ teaspoon sugar
1 teaspoon peanut oil
½ teaspoon white vinegar
½ teaspoon Shao-Hsing wine or sherry
Pinch of white pepper
1½ teaspoons cornstarch

For a sauce, combine in a bowl and mix well:
¼ teaspoon salt
1¼ teaspoons sugar
½ teaspoon sesame oil
1½ teaspoons cornstarch
1 teaspoon dark soy sauce
Pinch of white pepper
1 teaspoon white vinegar
2 teaspoons brown bean paste
¼ cup chicken broth

3 cups peanut oil
2 teaspoons minced ginger
2 teaspoons minced garlic
¼ cup julienne strips of Virginia ham
¼ cup bamboo shoots, cut into julienne
¾ cup fresh or frozen green peas
1 tablespoon Shao-Hsing wine or sherry

1. After washing shrimp, dry carefully, then allow to dry more thoroughly by leaving them in a single layer on wax paper for 2 to 3 hours. Turn over once during that time.

2. Wash watercress and break bunches into halves. Let drain, then blanch them in 8 cups water (see directions for water blanching, page 45). Place in a strainer, drain, and reserve.

3. Marinate pork for 30 minutes; reserve. Make the sauce; reserve.

4. Heat a wok over high heat for 40 seconds. Add peanut oil. When a wisp of white smoke appears, place shrimp in a Chinese strainer and oil-blanch for 1 minute (see directions for oil blanching, page 45). Remove and drain; reserve.

5. Empty wok of oil; replace 2 tablespoons oil. Over high heat add ginger; stir. Add garlic; stir. When garlic browns, add pork and marinade. Stir until meat becomes white. Add ham, bamboo shoots, and peas together, and mix with meat; cook for 2 minutes. Add shrimp. Stir together for 1 minute. Add wine and mix until blended.

6. Make a well in the mixture. Stir sauce and pour into the well. Mix all ingredients together, until sauce thickens. Turn off heat. Place watercress as a bed in a serving dish. Pour contents of wok over watercress and serve.

GORN
SIU
LOONG
HAR

Spicy Lobster

Lobster is rare in Szechuan because of its landlocked geographical position. This dish is very much a preparation for important banquets.

1 lobster, 2 pounds, freshly killed but not boiled, cut
    into 1½-inch-square pieces

For a marinade for the lobster, combine in a bowl and mix well:
    2 tablespoons white wine
    1 teaspoon white vinegar
    3 teaspoons light soy sauce
    1½ teaspoons sugar
    ¾ teaspoon salt
    1½ teaspoons sesame oil
    1½ tablespoons peanut oil
        Pinch of white pepper

3 tablespoons peanut oil

¼ cup shallots, cut into ¼-inch dice

2 teaspoons minced ginger

2 teaspoons minced garlic

For a sauce, combine in a bowl and mix well:

½ teaspoon dark soy sauce

¾ teaspoon sugar

1 teaspoon sesame oil

3½ tablespoons catsup

4 teaspoons cornstarch

⅓ cup chicken broth

1¼ teaspoons Hunan pepper sauce (see hot oil, page 20)

½ teaspoon hot oil

Pinch of white pepper

Sprigs of coriander

1. Marinate lobster for 30 minutes. Drain lobster. Reserve the marinade.

2. Heat a wok over high heat for 40 seconds. Add peanut oil and coat the wok with a spatula. Add shallots; let cook for 3 to 4 minutes, until they turn light brown. Add ginger; stir. Add garlic; stir. When garlic browns, add lobster pieces, spread in a thin layer. Tip wok from side to side to ensure thorough cooking.

3. Turn lobster pieces over; stir. If too dry, add the marinade. When lobster shells turn red, make a well in the center; stir and add the sauce. Stir all ingredients together thoroughly. When sauce thickens, remove lobster, place in a serving dish, garnish with sprigs of coriander, and serve.

SEI CHUN
CHAU
NGAU
YUK

Szechuan Beef

This is perhaps the best-known, the most universal of to-day's Chinese dishes. There are, however, many different versions of it, most of them sweetened, Westernized adaptations of the traditional Szechuan way of stir-frying beef. What follows is most traditional.

12 ounces "oyster cut" London broil

For marinade for beef, combine in a bowl and mix well:
   1 tablespoon oyster sauce
   1 teaspoon dark soy sauce
   1 teaspoon sesame oil
  ½ teaspoon salt
   1 teaspoon sugar
   2 teaspoons cornstarch
     Pinch of white pepper
  ½ teaspoon ginger juice mixed with 1 teaspoon
     Shao-Hsing wine or sherry

   1 medium-size carrot
  ½ small cucumber
  ½ medium-size green pepper
  ⅓ cup bamboo shoots
  ½ sweet red pepper
   1 large hot red pepper
1½ tablespoons julienne pieces of Szechuan mustard
     pickle
   1 tablespoon dried Chinese black mushrooms: soak in
     hot water for 30 minutes, wash, discard stems,
     cut into julienne
   3 tablespoons peanut oil
   1 slice of fresh ginger
  ½ teaspoon salt
   1 teaspoon sesame oil
   2 garlic cloves, minced
   2 teaspoons cornstarch mixed with 2 tablespoons cold
     water

1.   Slice beef into pieces 2 inches long, ½ inch wide. Slice thinly and evenly. Marinate for at least 1 hour.

2.   Wash and dry vegetables thoroughly; cut into thin matchstick-size pieces. Mince the hot pepper. Set aside.

3.   Brown vegetables: Pour 1½ tablespoons peanut oil into a preheated wok; add ginger and salt. When ginger browns slightly, add all vegetables. Stir-fry for 2 minutes and add sesame oil. Mix well, remove with a strainer, drain, and set aside.

4.   Wash wok with very hot water; rub clean lightly with brush or sponge. Place wok back on stove; dry with a paper towel. Heat remaining oil in the wok; add garlic and stir. When garlic browns, add meat. Spread in a thin layer, tipping wok from side to side, so meat browns evenly. Turn over and toss meat. When it changes color, add vegetables.

5.   Stir-fry meat and vegetables together. Make a well in the center and pour in cornstarch-water mixture. Cover with meat and vegetables and stir all together thoroughly for about 1 minute. Remove and serve immediately.

TUNG
GUA
YUNG

*Velvet
Wintermelon
Soup*

This is a most unusual recipe, simply because of the process of grating, then steaming the melon. I know of no other soup prepared quite like this.

3½ pounds wintermelon: peel, seed, grate

For steaming ingredients, combine:
  2 tablespoons white wine
  1 teaspoon salt
    Pinch of white pepper
  1 slice of ginger, ¼ inch thick
  2 teaspoons sugar

12 ounces chicken cutlets, chopped

For chicken marinade, combine in a bowl and mix well:

1 teaspoon ginger juice, mixed with 1 tablespoon white wine
3 teaspoons oyster sauce
3 teaspoons sesame oil
½ teaspoon salt
1 teaspoon sugar
4 teaspoons cornstarch
Pinch of white pepper
2 egg whites, beaten

5 cups chicken broth
⅓ cup scallions, green portions only, finely sliced

1.   Place grated wintermelon and steaming ingredients in a cake pan; place the pan in the bed of a bamboo steamer and set over boiling water in a wok. Cover and steam for 30 minutes (see steaming directions on page 46).

2.   As melon steams, marinate chicken for 20 minutes.

3.   In a large pot over high heat place chicken broth and steamed melon. Cover and bring to a boil. Add chicken and marinade, separating chicken pieces with a cooking spoon. Cook until chicken turns completely white, about 5 minutes.

4.   Add scallions. Turn off heat. Pour contents into a tureen and serve.

NOTE: This can be prepared 3 to 4 hours in advance of serving. Do not add scallions until just before serving.

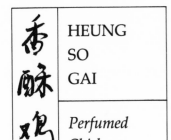

HEUNG
SO
GAI

*Perfumed
Chicken*

This lovely recipe illustrates a significant and often over-looked aspect of Szechuan cooking. Most people think that the cooking of Szechuan is all heat and spice, but it can be delicate and sophisticated, as you will see. There is an added bonus: If you add chopped vegetables to the cooking liquid, it becomes a wonderful soup.

1 whole fresh chicken, about 3½ pounds: wash,
    remove fat and membranes, dry, set aside
4 cups cold water
1 cup white wine
1 slice of fresh ginger
3 whole pieces of 8-star anise
¼ teaspoon Szechuan peppercorns
2 cinnamon sticks
¼ dried tangerine skin
2 scallions
2 teaspoons salt
2 teaspoons sugar
1 whole egg, beaten
¼ to ⅓ cup tapioca flour, sufficient to coat chicken
5 cups peanut oil

1. In a large oval Dutch oven place the chicken. Add next 10 ingredients, from water to sugar. Cover and bring to a boil. Add dark soy sauce, then cover pot and simmer for 20 minutes.

2. Turn chicken over and simmer for another 20 minutes. Remove chicken and allow to cool and dry for 4 to 5 hours, or refrigerate overnight.

3. Place chicken in a large dish, then coat with beaten egg. Place tapioca flour on a sheet of wax paper and coat chicken thoroughly by rolling it in tapioca flour. Set aside.

4. Heat a wok. Add peanut oil; bring oil to a boil. Place chicken in a large Chinese strainer and lower it into the oil to fry. Fry for 5 to 7 minutes, until it is golden brown. Remove, cut into bite-size pieces, and serve.

白	BOK
切	CHIT
肉	YUK
	White Cut Pork

The "white" in this justly famous Szechuan recipe refers to the plain water that is the basis for its cooking. It was taught to me by Chef Chan, the master cook of The Cleveland Restaurant, perhaps the best Szechuan kitchen in Hong Kong. The sauce is what helps to make it so special. White Cut Pork is always served cold.

  10 cups water
1½ teaspoons salt
  1 large onion: peel, cut into quarters
  1 slice of ginger
  1 whole garlic clove
  2 teaspoons sugar
2½ pounds pork, fresh ham, boned and skinned

1. In a large pot bring water to a boil. Add salt, onion, ginger, garlic, and sugar, then the piece of pork. Cover partially and simmer for 1½ to 2 hours, until a chopstick can be easily inserted into the meat. During the cooking process, turn the meat 4 or 5 times.

2. Remove pork from pot and put it into a large bowl of cold water. Allow it to rest there for 2 or 3 minutes. Remove and allow the meat to continue to cool. Wrap in plastic wrap and refrigerate on a dish.

3. When you are ready to serve, slice the meat paper-thin and arrange on a platter. Pour the hot sauce into a small bowl set in the middle of the platter.

BOK CHIT YUK JEUNG
White Cut Pork Sauce

Combine in a small bowl:

  2 tablespoons light soy sauce
  2 tablespoons dark soy sauce
½ teaspoon Hunan pepper sauce (see hot oil, page 20)
½ teaspoon sesame oil
  2 teaspoons white vinegar

1 teaspoon Shao-Hsing wine or sherry
2 teaspoons sugar
¾ teaspoon minced garlic
1 tablespoon minced scallion

NOTE: A serving suggestion: Alternate the white cut pork slices with thin, round, cross-cut slices of cucumber.

四 SEI
GUAI
DAU

季 *Four-Season Beans*

We Chinese call these four-season beans simply because green string beans are available to us throughout the year.

3 tablespoons fresh pork, cut into ⅛-inch dice

For marinade for pork, combine in a bowl:
½ teaspoon sesame oil
¼ teaspoon sugar
⅛ teaspoon white vinegar
⅛ teaspoon Shao-Hsing wine or sherry
¼ teaspoon cornstarch
¼ teaspoon light soy sauce

3 cups peanut oil
12 ounces fresh green string beans: remove both ends, wash, dry very thoroughly because they are to be oil-blanched
2 teaspoons minced ginger
2 teaspoons minced garlic

For sauce, combine in a bowl and mix well:
1 teaspoon dark soy sauce
½ teaspoon sugar
½ teaspoon sesame oil
½ teaspoon white vinegar
½ teaspoon Shao-Hsing wine or sherry
1 teaspoon cornstarch
3 tablespoons chicken broth
Pinch of white pepper

1.   Marinate pork for 30 minutes.

2.   Heat a wok over high heat for 40 seconds. Add peanut oil. When a wisp of white smoke appears, lower beans into oil with a Chinese strainer and oil-blanch for 2 minutes or until beans soften (see directions for oil-blanching, page 45). Remove with a strainer and drain over a bowl.

3.   Pour off oil from wok. Replace 1½ tablespoons oil in the wok. Over high heat add ginger and stir; add garlic and stir. When garlic browns, add pork and marinade and mix well. When pork turns white add the beans and stir, cooking for about 3 minutes.

4.   Make a well in center. Stir the sauce, then pour it into the well. Mix all ingredients thoroughly. When sauce thickens, remove from wok and serve.

SEI
CHUN
JIN
YUE

*Szechuan
Panfried Fish*

1 whole striped bass, 2½ pounds: clean thoroughly inside and out, remove intestines and extra fat, wash the fish inside and out, dry well

For a seasoning mixture, combine well:
  2 teaspoons salt
  ¼ teaspoon white pepper
  2 tablespoons white wine
  4 large slices of ginger, shredded

4 tablespoons peanut oil
1 teaspoon sesame oil
2 garlic cloves, whole

For pork mixture, combine and reserve:
  2 tablespoons shredded pork
  ½ teaspoon sesame oil

1 large hot pepper, finely sliced
12 tiger lily buds: soak, discard hard ends, cut into halves
4 large dried Chinese black mushrooms: soak, wash, discard stems, shred

For a sauce, combine in a bowl and mix well:
> 1 teaspoon salt
> ½ teaspoon sugar
> 1½ tablespoons oyster sauce
> 1 tablespoon dark soy sauce
>   Pinch of white pepper
> 3½ tablespoons cornstarch
> 1½ cups water or chicken broth

2 cakes of fresh bean curd: dry well, slice into ¼-inch pieces
2 large scallions, white portions only: wash, dry, shred

1. Rub fish inside and out thoroughly with seasoning mixture. Allow to stand for 20 minutes, then gently pat dry.

2. Pour 3 tablespoons peanut oil and the sesame oil into a wok. Add garlic. Coat wok. When white smoke appears, place fish in oil and fry, tipping wok toward fire so fish cooks evenly. Fry fish for 5 minutes. Turn over with spatula and cook for 7 to 10 minutes longer. Remove fish and place in a 250° F. oven to keep warm. Clean the wok.

3. Pour remaining 1 tablespoon peanut oil into the wok and heat until white smoke appears. Add pork mixture; brown. Add sliced hot pepper and stir together. Add tiger lily buds, mushrooms, and ½ cup cold water; cook until mushrooms are tender. Add the sauce and stir, mixing until it becomes thick and dark. Water may be added if the mixture becomes too thick.

4. Add fresh bean curd slices and stir into mixture briefly. Add scallions and stir in briefly. Remove fish from the oven, pour over it the mixed contents of the wok, and serve immediately.

NOTE: This fish can be prepared 2 to 3 hours in advance. It can be reheated in a preheated 325° F. oven for 15 to 20 minutes, or until fish is hot. If prepared in advance, the sauce should be prepared just before serving and poured over the fish at that time.

A BANQUET FROM HUNAN

LOT YEH CHOI	*Peppery Cabbage*
HUNAN LOT HAR	*Hunan Spicy Shrimp*
HUNAN JIU LOT GAI	*Hunan Pepper Chicken*
CHUN PEI NGAU YUK	*Orange Beef*
LO GEUNG YUK PIN TONG	*Ginger Soup*
YUE HUNG YUK SEE	*Shredded Pork with Garlic Sauce*
SIUM BAU YUNG YUK	*Stir-Fried Leeks with Lamb*
YUE HUNG KEH TZI	*Eggplant with Garlic Sauce*
SOH JAH SEH BARN	*Hot and Crisp Fish*

辣椰菜	LOT YEH CHOI
	Peppery Cabbage

Cabbage is such a familiar vegetable to Westerners that I am often asked by my students if it really exists in China. It does indeed. In Canton, where I grew up, there were miles and miles of it in the fields, and we ate it in soup and stir-fried because it was so sweet. It was in America that I learned that cabbage could be turned into something called coleslaw. What I have done is to use the flavors of western China, of Hunan and Szechuan, to create a hot, spicy coleslawlike dish.

    2 pounds cabbage, cut into pieces 1 by ½ inch
1¼ teaspoons salt
    ½ sweet red pepper, cut into ¼-inch slices
    2 tablespoons sugar
4½ tablespoons white vinegar
        Pinch of white pepper
2½ tablespoons corn oil
  10 small dried hot peppers

1.   In a large bowl mix cabbage with salt and allow to sit for 2 hours. Drain off all liquid.

2.   Add red pepper, sugar, vinegar, and white pepper, and mix.

3.   Pour oil into a wok over high heat and add dried hot peppers. Stir-fry until peppers turn dark brown or black. Add to cabbage mixture; mix well.

4.   Refrigerate for 24 hours before serving.

NOTE: Amount of hot pepper can be varied to taste.

HUNAN
LOT
HAR

*Hunan Spicy
Shrimp*

This versatile preparation can be served hot or cold. Its spicy, sweet flavor is distinctive. If it is to be eaten hot, I suggest it be accompanied by some plain cooked rice. Cold, it can be one of two first courses in a banquet, served directly after the Peppery Cabbage.

3 to 4 cups peanut oil
1¼ pounds shrimp: shell, devein, leave tail portions on, wash, dry, refrigerate for at least 4 hours
½ cup onions, diced into ¼-inch pieces
2 tablespoons finely chopped fresh ginger
1 garlic clove, minced

For a sauce, combine in a bowl and mix well:
1½ tablespoons oyster sauce
3 teaspoons sugar
4 tablespoons catsup
1 teaspoon salt
Pinch of white pepper
2 teaspoons Hunan pepper

1 teaspoon sesame oil

1. Pour peanut oil into a wok and heat to 375° F. Oil-blanch the shrimp for 45 seconds to 1 minute, until shrimp begin to turn pink and to curl. (See oil-blanching technique, page 45.) Remove; set aside.

2. Remove oil from wok, then replace 2 tablespoons oil. Heat oil until white smoke appears. Add onions, ginger, and garlic, and stir-fry until onions soften, about 2 minutes. Add shrimp and toss together thoroughly. Stir sauce and pour into the wok. Stir together until shrimp are well coated.

3. Add sesame oil, turn off heat, and stir well. Remove from wok and serve immediately.

NOTE: This may be served cold, as I mentioned, or alone as an appetizer.

HUNAN
JIU
LOT
GAI

Hunan Pepper Chicken

2 chicken legs with thighs, each 8 ounces: bone, remove fat, membranes, and skin, wash thoroughly and cut into bite-size pieces, dry very well
1 egg, beaten
¼ teaspoon salt
Pinch of white pepper
2 teaspoons cornstarch

For a sauce, combine in a bowl and mix well:
4 teaspoons dark soy sauce
1 garlic clove, minced
1 slice of fresh ginger, cut into small pieces
2 teaspoons hoisin sauce
1 teaspoon sugar
1 teaspoon white vinegar
½ teaspoon Shao-Hsing wine or sherry

3½ cups peanut oil
2 tablespoons scallions, white portions, cut into ⅛-inch slices
8 to 10 small dried hot chili peppers

1. Marinate chicken pieces in beaten egg, salt, pepper, and 1 teaspoon cornstarch for 5 minutes. Reserve.

2. Make sauce and reserve it.

3. Heat a wok over high heat for 40 seconds; add peanut oil. When wisp of white smoke appears, oil is ready. Sprinkle remaining teaspoon of cornstarch over chicken pieces and place them in the hot oil. Deep-fry for 1½ to 2 minutes, until chicken is crisp. Drain.

4. Empty wok of oil and place back over heat. When residue of oil heats up, add scallions and chili peppers. Stir for about 40 seconds. Add chicken and stir until well mixed.

5. Stir sauce and add to wok. Mix all ingredients until chicken pieces are thoroughly coated with sauce, about 3 minutes. There should be no liquid in the wok. Remove and serve immediately.

CHUN
PEI
NGAU
YUK

Orange Beef

This is justly one of the most famous dishes of Hunan, one that has found a great deal of favor in the United States. It is subject to small variations because each chef believes *his* way of making it is distinctive, and each chef guards his version jealously. It is most often cooked with dried orange peel. I prefer fresh orange peel, for two reasons: As it cooks, the aroma of orange is striking and pleasing, and as it is eaten the occasional tastes of bits of fresh peel are refreshing.

    8 ounces flank steak, weighed after trimming, cut into
        strips ¼ inch by 2½ inches
    ½ teaspoon baking soda
    1 tablespoon egg white, lightly beaten
    ¼ teaspoon Shao-Hsing wine or sherry
        Pinch of white pepper
    1 tablespoon peanut oil
    1½ tablespoons cornstarch
    1 fresh hot red pepper, minced
    1 scallion: cut off both ends, wash, dry, cut into ½-inch
        pieces
    2 teaspoons minced fresh ginger
    1 teaspoon minced garlic
    5 dried chili peppers
    1½ tablespoons fresh orange peel, cut into pieces ⅛ by ½
        inch

    For sauce, combine in a bowl and mix well:
    2 teaspoons dark soy sauce
    1 tablespoon sugar
    1 teaspoon sesame oil
    1 teaspoon white vinegar
    2 tablespoons chicken broth
        Pinch of white pepper

    3½ cups peanut oil
    6 slices of fresh orange

1. Marinate flank steak with the baking soda in the refrigerator overnight. After marinating, wash beef thoroughly, at least twice, with cold water to remove any residue of baking soda. Drain off water.

2. Place beef in a bowl, add egg white, and mix well until beef is well coated with egg white. Add wine, white pepper, 1 tablespoon peanut oil, and the cornstarch; mix with your hand each time an ingredient is added. Let stand for 1 hour. There should be no residue.

3. Have the vegetables and orange peel ready. Have the sauce ready.

4. Heat a wok over high heat for 1 minute. Add peanut oil and heat to 400° to 425° F. Place strips of beef, one by one, in the oil and cook for 1½ minutes. Keep loosening beef with a ladle. Remove meat with a strainer and drain. Reserve.

5. Heat oil again to 400° to 425° F. Place beef again in oil. Cook for 2 minutes, until beef becomes crisp on the outside. Remove and let drain.

6. Drain off oil from the wok. Replace 1 tablespoon oil in wok, and heat over high heat. Add dried chili peppers; stir. Then add all vegetables and mix together for 1½ minutes. Add beef again. Let cook for 45 seconds.

7. Stir the sauce, make a well in the mixture, pour in the sauce. Mix until the sauce evaporates and beef acquires a shiny coating. Remove to a serving dish; garnish with slices of fresh orange.

LO
GEUNG
YUK
PIN
TONG

Ginger Soup

What makes this traditional Hunanese soup so unusual is that it is based on ginger, a circumstance that as far as I know is unique to that Chinese province. It is also delicious.

12 ounces lean pork, thinly sliced into pieces ½ by 1½ inches

For marinade for pork, combine in a bowl and mix well:
   1 egg white, beaten
   3 teaspoons cornstarch
   2 teaspoons sesame seed oil
1½ teaspoons Shao-Hsing wine or sherry
   2 teaspoons white vinegar
   ¼ teaspoon salt
2½ teaspoons sugar
   Pinch of white pepper

5½ cups chicken broth
  2 cups cold water
2½ tablespoons fresh ginger, cut into ½-inch-square pieces
  2 tablespoons cloud ears: soak in hot water for 30 minutes, wash, reserve
  3 tablespoons Szechuan Mustard Pickle: slice into pieces ¼ by 1 inch
  1 cup snow peas: remove strings and both ends, wash, cut into ¼-inch julienne
  2 scallions: discard both ends, wash, dry, cut into ½-inch diagonal pieces
  3 teaspoons sesame oil

1. Marinate pork for 30 minutes. Reserve.

2. Place chicken broth and water in a large pot over high heat, cover, and bring to a boil. Add ginger, cloud ears, and mustard pickle; bring back to a boil, lower heat, and cover. Let cook for 7 minutes.

3.   Turn heat to high. Add pork and marinade; stir, separating pork with a wooden spoon. Let the soup come back to a boil for 3 to 5 minutes, covered, then add snow peas and scallions and allow to return to a boil. Turn off heat. Add sesame oil and stir to mix it well into the soup. Pour into a soup tureen and serve immediately.

NOTE: This soup can be made ahead, but snow peas, scallions, and sesame seed oil must be left until the final stages of reheating.

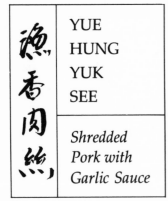

YUE
HUNG
YUK
SEE

*Shredded
Pork with
Garlic Sauce*

The use of garlic-based sauces is widespread in Hunan. The flavor of garlic is blended with fish, meat, vegetables, and surprisingly displays a good deal of versatility. For example, this recipe and the one that follows both have garlic sauces, but they are quite different indeed.

12 ounces lean fresh pork, loin preferred, shredded

For a marinade for pork, combine in a bowl and mix well:
½ egg white, beaten
¼ teaspoon salt
½ teaspoon sugar
1 teaspoon white vinegar
1 teaspoon sherry or Shao-Hsing wine
1½ teaspoons peanut oil
½ teaspoon sesame oil
2 teaspoons cornstarch
   Pinch of white pepper

For a sauce, combine in a bowl and mix well:
1 teaspoon minced garlic
1½ tablespoons catsup
   Pinch of white pepper
   Pinch of ground Szechuan pepper
2 teaspoons sugar
2 teaspoons white vinegar
2 teaspoons Shao-Hsing wine or sherry
2 teaspoons preserved horse beans with chili
1½ teaspoons cornstarch
2½ tablespoons minced scallions
2 teaspoons minced ginger
3 tablespoons chicken broth

4 cups water
½ teaspoon baking soda
2 bunches of watercress: wash, break into halves, drain

3 tablespoons peanut oil
5 cups peanut oil for oil-blanching
1 teaspoon minced garlic
⅓ cup bamboo shoots, shredded
2 fresh water chestnuts: peel, wash, dry, cut into
    julienne
¼ cup shredded sweet red pepper

1. Marinate pork for 30 minutes. Reserve. Make the sauce; reserve.

2. Pour the water into a large pot, add baking soda, and bring to a boil. Add watercress. Using chopsticks, turn until watercress is completely submerged in water. When it turns bright green, remove, drain through a strainer, and set aside.

3. Heat a wok over high heat for 1 minute. Add 1½ tablespoons of peanut oil and coat the wok with a spatula. Stir-fry watercress for about 2 minutes, or until coated with oil. Remove and spread out on a serving dish.

4. Clean wok with a paper towel. Reheat, add 5 cups peanut oil, and heat to 325° F. Using a strainer, lower the pork into the oil to blanch it (see oil-blanching directions, page 45). When pork turns white, remove and drain.

5. Empty wok of oil. Add remaining 1½ tablespoons peanut oil to wok over high heat. Coat wok with a spatula. When a wisp of white smoke appears, add garlic. When it browns, add bamboo shoots and water chestnuts and mix well. Add sweet pepper and mix. Return pork to wok and combine all thoroughly.

6. Make a well in the mixture. Stir sauce and add to wok; combine all ingredients. When sauce thickens, remove pork and vegetables from the wok and pour over the bed of watercress. Serve immediately.

NOTE: The watercress may be used as a side dish if preferred.

SIUM BAU
YUNG
YUK

*Stir-Fried
Leeks with
Lamb*

This vegetable, almost a staple in France, is also somewhat familiar in the western and northern parts of China as well as in its prime vegetable-growing area in Canton. It is often stir-fried with shrimp or beef, but in Hunan it is traditionally served with lamb.

8 ounces lamb, weighed after trimming, leg fillet
    recommended: cut into slices 1½ by 2 inches

For a marinade for lamb, combine in a bowl and mix well:
  2 teaspoons sesame oil
  1 teaspoon peanut oil
 4½ teaspoons dark soy sauce
  1 teaspoon Shao-Hsing wine or sherry
  ¾ teaspoon white vinegar
 1½ teaspoons sugar
 1¾ teaspoons cornstarch
    Pinch of white pepper

2½ tablespoons peanut oil
  8 ounces leeks: wash, remove both ends, cut into
    sections ¼ inch wide by 1½ inches long
1½ teaspoons garlic
  4 teaspoons minced ginger
  2 teaspoons Shao-Hsing wine or sherry

For a sauce, combine in a bowl and mix well:
  ¼ teaspoon salt
  ½ teaspoon sugar
  1 teaspoon cornstarch
  ½ teaspoon white vinegar
  ½ teaspoon Shao-Hsing wine or sherry
    Pinch of white pepper
  3 tablespoons chicken broth

1 teaspoon sesame oil

1.   Marinate lamb for 1 hour. Reserve.

2.   Heat a wok over high heat for 1 minute. Add 1 table-spoon peanut oil. Add leeks, stir-fry for 30 seconds, remove, and set aside.

3.   Wipe off wok and spatula with dry paper towel. Heat the wok over high heat again for 1 minute, add remaining peanut oil, and coat the sides of the wok with a spatula. When a wisp of white smoke appears, add the garlic and ginger; stir. When garlic is brown, add lamb and its marinade.

4.   Spread meat in a single layer. Cook for 1 minute; turn over. Add wine around edge of wok; stir. Add reserved leeks and stir.

5.   Make a well in the center of the mixture. Stir sauce and pour it in. Mix thoroughly. Turn off heat. Add sesame oil. Mix well, place on serving dish, and serve immediately.

YUE
HUNG
KEH
TZI

Eggplant with Garlic Sauce

3 cups peanut oil
1 pound eggplant: peel, slice lengthwise into ½-inch
    strips
2 teaspoons minced garlic

For a sauce, combine in a bowl and mix well:
   1 tablespoon dark soy sauce
   ½ teaspoon Hunan pepper
   2 teaspoons sugar
   2 teaspoons oyster sauce
   1 teaspoon white vinegar
   ¼ teaspoon salt
   ½ teaspoon cornstarch mixed with 2 teaspoons
       chicken broth
   ½ teaspoon Shao-Hsing wine or sherry

1.   Heat a wok over high heat for 45 seconds. Add peanut oil. Heat until a wisp of white smoke appears. Place eggplant strips in a strainer and lower into oil. Cook for 1 minute, or until eggplant softens. Remove, drain, reserve.

2.   Empty oil from wok. Return 1½ tablespoons oil to the wok. Raise heat and add minced garlic. Stir until it browns, then again place eggplant in the wok. Stir together and cook for 1½ minutes more.

3.   Make a well in the center of the mixture. Stir sauce and pour it in. Stir until sauce thickens. Remove and serve.

SOH
JAH
SEH
BARN

*Hot and
Crisp Fish*

1½ to 1¾ pounds sea bass: clean, remove membranes,
    wash and dry thoroughly
1½ teaspoons white vinegar
 2 tablespoons white wine
 1 teaspoon salt
 ¼ teaspoon white pepper
 ½ cup cornstarch
5½ cups peanut oil
 ½ cup ¼-inch dice of onions
 1 tablespoon minced ginger
 2 small hot red peppers, minced
 2 tablespoons ¼-inch dice of carrot
 2 tablespoons ¼-inch dice of bamboo shoots

For a sauce, combine in a bowl and mix well:
   2 tablespoons sugar
   ½ teaspoon salt
   2 tablespoons white vinegar
   2 tablespoons sherry
   1 tablespoon dark soy sauce
  1½ teaspoons cornstarch

¼ cup chicken broth
¼ cup catsup
1 teaspoon sesame oil
½ teaspoon Szechuan Chili Paste
2 tablespoons sweet wine rice (see page 230)
   Pinch of white pepper

2 tablespoons ¼-inch pieces of scallions
   Sprigs of coriander

1.   Place thoroughly dry fish in a dish. Cut 5 slits diagonally into the fish's side, repeat on other side, but do not cut through to bone. Sprinkle with white vinegar all over, inside and out. Repeat with white wine. Repeat with salt. Repeat with white pepper. Place cornstarch on a sheet of wax paper and coat bass with it thoroughly on both sides, including the opening made for cleaning.

2.   Heat a wok over high heat for 40 seconds. Pour oil into the wok and heat to 375° to 400° F. Place fish in a Chinese strainer and lower into the oil. (If fish cannot be lowered completely into oil, use a ladle to baste it with oil, and tip strainer so the fish is completely cooked, including the head.) Fry for 10 to 12 minutes, until cooked. Remove and drain. Reserve.

3.   Empty oil from wok, replace 1½ tablespoons oil, and heat. Add onions; cook for 5 minutes. Add ginger, mix, cook for 30 seconds. Then add peppers, carrot, and bamboo shoots. Add sauce and combine all ingredients thoroughly. Cook until sauce thickens.

4.   Place fish in a serving dish. Pour sauce over it and top with scallions. Garnish with coriander and serve.

NOTE: If sea bass is unobtainable, a flounder of the same weight will substitute nicely. If a flounder is used, cut the cooking time by 3 or 4 minutes.

A B A N Q U E T O F T H E H A K K A

YUNG DAU FU	*Stuffed Bean Curd Hakka Style*
BOK SOI HAR	*White Water Shrimp*
YIM GUK GAI	*Salt-Baked Chicken*
MUI CHOI KAU YUK	*Preserved Vegetables with Fresh Bacon*
SAI YEUNG CHOI YUK YEUN TONG	*Watercress Soup with Meatballs*
BOT BOH CHEUN OP	*Eight-Jewel Stuffed Duck*
HOM SOON CHOI CHAU NGAU YUK	*Beef and Sour Mustard Pickle*
HOK BOK TUNG GU	*Black and White Mushrooms*
HAKKA LIN BAU FON	*Lotus Leaf Rice, Hakka-Style*

HAKKA
Cooking of the Nomads

The Hakka are perhaps the most romantic of Chinese people. They are China's historic wanderers who traveled south from the area known as Mongolia, settling finally in the area around Canton and in Hong Kong's New Territories. Often persecuted, the Hakka became insular, and even to this day they keep to themselves a good deal. If you visit Hong Kong or southern China you may recognize them by their distinctive dress—shiny black cotton pajamas and wide-brimmed hats with cloth fringes hanging down. Though they are insular, as I have said, they are not reclusive. They are keen business people; their capacity for work is prodigious. They were the Chinese who settled Hawaii. Their cooking is quite distinctive.

Because they were nomads they often ate as they traveled. They had no permanent homes, no permanent stoves. They ate what they caught from the sea, or raised in herds, or grew. And they ate everything, wasting nothing.

Their most famous dish is salt-baked chicken, and it is a marvel of ingenuity. How to bake without an oven? They dug a hole in the ground, lined it with stones, made a bed of readily available sea salt, set the chicken in it, covered it with more salt, and created an "oven." When they killed a pig, my grandmother used to say, they ate everything including its whiskers. They preserved vegetables so they could be portable. They boiled them and then flavored them with cold sauces that did not have to be heated. They boiled soybeans and ate the curds from it.

The Hakka repertory is quite limited, but when the wanderers settled in south China they gradually adopted quite a few Cantonese preparations. These days the Hakka cook what is a combination of their own traditional foods and those they have adopted in Canton. Their food is rarely available in the United States. Often, what is presented as Hakka cooking is not that at all, but somebody's idea of what it is supposed to be. In this book you will find authentic Hakka dishes prepared the way the Hakka prepare them. I have made a few changes for the American kitchen, but none in spirit.

YUNG
DAU
FU

*Stuffed
Bean Curd
Hakka Style*

I prefer that you use Chinese bean curd rather than Japanese or Korean for this dish, because its texture is smoother and softer. As I've said, bean curd should always be purchased fresh, and stored in a container of fresh water, refrigerated. It will remain fresh for 2 to 3 weeks if the water is changed daily.

6 cakes fresh bean curd
6 ounces shrimp: shell, devein, wash, dry

For shrimp filling, combine in a bowl and mix well:
½ teaspoon ginger juice mixed with 1½ teaspoons white wine
½ teaspoon light soy sauce
1 teaspoon sesame oil
2 teaspoons oyster sauce
¼ teaspoon salt
¾ teaspoon sugar
½ egg, beaten
Pinch of white pepper
1½ tablespoons cornstarch
3 scallions, finely chopped

To make the sauce, combine in a bowl and mix well:
1 tablespoon oyster sauce
1 tablespoon dark soy sauce
1 tablespoon cornstarch
¼ teaspoon salt
½ teaspoon sugar
1 cup chicken broth or cold water

1 tablespoon tapioca flour
4 tablespoons peanut oil
4 scallions: discard both ends, wash, dry, cut into 1½-inch sections

1. Remove bean curd from water, place in a strainer over a bowl, and allow to drain for 3 to 4 hours. Pat dry with a paper towel.

2. Chop shrimp into a paste, add to bowl of filling ingredients, and mix thoroughly. Refrigerate for 2 hours.

3. Mix sauce and reserve.

4. Cut each cake of bean curd diagonally; with a pointed knife, cut out a pocket in each half of the curd.

5. Dust the pocket with tapioca flour, then fill with a tablespoon of the shrimp mixture. Pack smoothly with a knife or with your fingers.

6. Stuffed bean curd may be cooked in any of the following ways: Steam for 8 to 10 minutes, until shrimp turn pink in color.

    or

    Deep-fry, 2 or 3 at a time, in peanut oil heated to 325° F., for about 8 minutes, until the curd is golden brown.

    or

    Pour 2 to 3 tablespoons peanut oil into a cast-iron skillet. Heat over high heat until a wisp of white smoke appears. With the stuffed side of the bean curd down, panfry over medium heat for 6 minutes. Turn curds and cook each side for 2 minutes. After cooking, place in a serving dish and keep in a warm oven.

7. Heat a wok, pour in 1 tablespoon peanut oil, and heat until a wisp of smoke appears. Add scallions, and cook for 45 seconds, until they become bright green. Lower heat; remove and reserve scallions.

8. Stir the sauce and pour into the wok; stir with a spatula. Turn heat to medium high; continue stirring until sauce thickens and turns dark brown. (Raise heat if sauce is not thickening.) Place scallions in sauce. Stir together. Pour over bean curd and serve immediately.

BOK
SOI
HAR

White Water Shrimp

These are called "white water" shrimp because they are in fact poached in boiling water, one of a very few such recipes and one that illustrates a simple and delicious preparation that could be cooked by the Hakkas while they were on the move.

1 pound medium shrimp, 25 to 30: wash, leave shells on
3 cups cold water
¼ cup white wine
2 scallions: wash, discard both ends, mash white
       portion lightly, cut into 3 sections
1 slice of ginger, ½ inch thick, lightly mashed
4 fresh basil leaves
6 fresh mint leaves
1 garlic clove, peeled and mashed
3 small fresh chili peppers
1 tablespoon sugar
2 teaspoons salt
1 tablespoon scallion oil (see page 24)

To make the sauce, combine in a bowl and mix well:
1½ tablespoons light soy sauce
  2 small chili peppers, thinly sliced
  1 teaspoon scallion oil
  ½ teaspoon sesame oil
  ½ teaspoon white vinegar
    Pinch of white pepper

1. Squeeze shrimp about ½ inch from top and vein will pop out. Pull gently out of the body.

2. Place all ingredients except shrimp in a large heavy pot, such as a cast aluminum pot. Bring to a boil over high heat. Allow to boil for 2 minutes.

3. Add shrimp and bring back to a boil. Turn off heat, place cover on pot, and let mixture sit for 3 to 5 minutes, until shrimp turn pink and curl up. Remove and serve with sauce.

NOTE: Sauce should be made 1 to 2 hours before serving, so that ingredients will have an opportunity to blend.

盐焗鸡	YIM GUK GAI
	Salt-Baked Chicken

This is perhaps the most famous dish of the Hakka people. The salt used in its preparation does not make the chicken salty. It is, rather, the oven that cooks the chicken. The Hakka, because they were nomads, had no ovens, so they would dig a shallow hole in the ground, place stones in it, then create an "oven" out of sea salt. I have re-created this process with salt in a Dutch oven.

Sad to say, you will seldom get genuine salt-baked chicken in restaurants, even those which call themselves Hakka. In most cases the chicken is thrust into a series of boiling salt solutions to cook and it is presented as salt-baked. It is better, more satisfying, more delicious, to make your own.

1   whole chicken, 3 to 3¼ pounds
2   scallions: wash, dry
½   teaspoon powdered sand ginger mixed with 1 tablespoon Shao-Hsing wine or sherry
1   slice of fresh ginger, ¼ inch thick
¼   dried tangerine skin: soak in hot water for 30 minutes, until soft
4½   pounds kosher salt

Special tools
1   piece of cheesecloth, 4 feet long

1.   Clean and wash chicken; remove fat and membranes. Drain off excess water, allow chicken to drain thoroughly, and pat dry with paper towels.

2.   Remove both ends of scallions. Smash the scallions with the flat of the cleaver blade; cut each one into 4 equal pieces. Set aside.

3.   Rub wine-ginger mixture inside chicken cavity and around outside as well. Place scallions, ginger, and tangerine skin inside chicken. Wrap with cheesecloth.

4.   Preheat oven to 450° F.

5. Heat a wok, add salt, and dry-roast over high heat until salt is very hot. Scoop half of salt into a Dutch oven, place wrapped chicken firmly into the bed, then add the rest of the salt, making sure the entire chicken is covered. Roast uncovered for 1 hour and 10 minutes. Remove from oven; let sit for 15 minutes.

Scoop salt into a Dutch oven.

6. Remove chicken to a large platter. Unwrap it; discard cheesecloth. Chop chicken into bite-size pieces. Serve with a sauce.

Salt-Baked Chicken Sauce
   3 tablespoons light soy sauce
   2 tablespoons scallion oil (see page 24)
   1 teaspoon sesame oil
   1 teaspoon Chinese red vinegar
1½ tablespoons finely shredded ginger
1½ tablespoons finely shredded white portions of
      scallion
   Pinch of white pepper

Mix all ingredients together and serve in a small decorative bowl.

MUI
CHOI
KAU
YUK

*Preserved
Vegetables with
Fresh Bacon*

This is truly a Hakka-only dish; it is to be found nowhere else in China. To many Westerners the very idea of eating fresh bacon, with its goodly amount of fat, is a bit unpleasant. However, the cooking process removes any cloying aspects and the bacon is cooked thoroughly and deliciously. My husband, who trims every imaginable bit of fat from his meats, tasted this for the first time and found it to be absolutely wonderful. Which it is, perhaps because I boil the fresh bacon rather than fry it, as many Hakka people do.

4 ounces preserved vegetable
2 to 2½ pounds fresh, uncured bacon, in one piece
8 cups cold water
5 ounces sugar cane sugar or dark brown sugar
3 tablespoons Shao-Hsing wine or sherry
1 cup mushroom soy sauce

1. Wash preserved vegetable carefully: Remove each stalk and open leaves to allow sand and salt to wash off. Repeat 4 times.

2. In a large, oval Dutch oven place all ingredients except the mushroom soy sauce. Bring to a boil over high heat. Add mushroom soy sauce and bring back to a boil. Cover, reduce heat, and allow to simmer for 4 hours. Use a chopstick to test the bacon. If chopstick goes into the bacon easily, it is done. If not, cook for another 30 minutes to 1 hour. When meat is done, allow pot to cool.

3. Remove meat and vegetables to a large dish. Allow to cool to room temperature, then cover and refrigerate for 8 hours or overnight. Reserve 1 cup of the cooking liquid. It is to be added later to give the bacon a rich, dark color.

4. Remove vegetables from dish, cut into ⅛-inch slices, and make a bed of them in a heatproof dish. Slice bacon across into ⅓-inch pieces. Reassemble slices and place atop vegetable. Coat bacon with as much of the reserved cooking liquid as is necessary to give it a dark coating. Steam for 30 minutes. Serve immediately with cooked white rice.

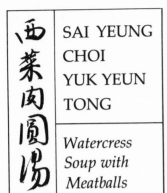

SAI YEUNG CHOI YUK YEUN TONG

Watercress Soup with Meatballs

Beef balls are quite common in Hakka cooking, as are balls of fish. Unfortunately, in most instances the meatballs become dense, hard, almost springy after being boiled in the soup. I have altered the recipe slightly to make them more tender.

For meatballs, combine:
1 pound ground beef chuck
½ teaspoon salt
½ teaspoon sugar
2 teaspoons light soy sauce
2 teaspoons oyster sauce
1 teaspoon Shao-Hsing wine or sherry
1 teaspoon sesame oil
4 teaspoons cornstarch
1 egg white, beaten

3½ cups chicken broth
3½ cups water
½ teaspoon baking soda
1 slice of ginger
4 large bunches of watercress: wash thoroughly, break each stem with leaves into 3 equal pieces

1. Stir the meatball ingredients in a bowl clockwise, with chopsticks, until quite soft and well blended. If mixture is too moist, add another teaspoon of cornstarch. Several times, as you are mixing the meat, pick up the entire mass and slap it down hard into the bowl. This ensures that the meatballs will not fall apart when cooking. Form meat into 30 or 40 small balls. Set aside.

2. Pour chicken broth and water into a pot. Add baking soda and ginger and bring to a boil.

3. Add meatballs; bring liquid to a boil again. When meatballs float to the top, they are cooked. Raise the heat.

4. Add watercress; bring soup to a boil again. Pour into a tureen and serve immediately.

NOTE: Watercress must *always* be cooked in boiling liquid, otherwise it will be excessively bitter.

八寶全鴨

BOT
BOH
CHEUN
OP

*Eight-Jewel
Stuffed Duck*

This is an important, symbolic preparation. The duck must be stuffed with eight ingredients and only eight, to represent the eight immortals of Taoism, the eight auspicious signs of Buddha, the eight organs of Buddha's body, the eight famous horses of Mu Wang of the Chou dynasty, the eight paths to everlasting happiness It seems to be placing an awful lot of symbolism on a single stuffed duck, but that is the truth of it.

1 duck, 4 to 4½ pounds
¾ cup lotus seeds
8 ounces shrimp: wash, shell, devein, cut into ¼-inch
    dice

For the marinade for shrimp, combine in a bowl and mix well:
½ teaspoon ginger juice mixed with 1 teaspoon
    sherry
1¼ teaspoons salt
2¼ teaspoons sugar
½ teaspoon light soy sauce
1 teaspoon white vinegar
1 teaspoon sesame oil
1 tablespoon oyster sauce
1 teaspoon cornstarch
    Pinch of white pepper

1½ tablespoons peanut oil
1 teaspoon minced ginger
2 teaspoons white vinegar
3 teaspoons Shao-Hsing wine or sherry
3 cups glutinous rice
3 cups chicken broth
½ cup fresh water chestnuts: peel, wash, cut into ¼-
    inch dice
½ cup dried Chinese black mushrooms, 6 to 8: soak in
    hot water for 30 minutes, wash, discard stems,
    cut into ¼-inch dice
8 scallions: discard both ends, wash, dry, slice finely

¾ cup bamboo shoots, cut into ¼-inch dice
2 tablespoons oyster sauce
1 tablespoon sesame oil
2 teaspoons light soy sauce
2 teaspoons dark soy sauce
2 teaspoons sugar
2 teaspoons minced garlic
Pinch of white pepper
2 tablespoons dark soy sauce, to coat duck before
    roasting

1. Bone the duck. Boning is a bit tricky. The object is to remove the bones, but to keep the meat and skin intact. Here are detailed instructions:

Set the bird upright, almost in a sitting position. Using a cleaver, cut off head and neck and reserve. With a paring knife loosen and remove fat and gristle around the neck area. Keep skin and meat intact.

Cut into wing joint to loosen, and detach wishbone from breastbone. These are all in the same spot and you have to work around with care. Work the whole wishbone out of the bird.

Work to remove "shoulder blade" and small back bones from spinal column.

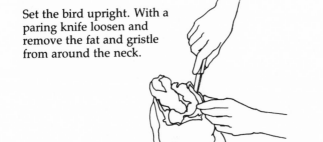

Set the bird upright. With a paring knife loosen and remove the fat and gristle from around the neck.

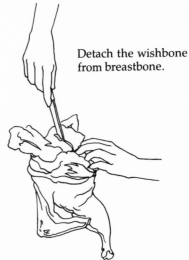

Detach the wishbone from breastbone.

Detach rib cage from breast plate, teasing the meat from the bone.

Slowly detach skin from the back, working your way toward the legs.

Detach rib-cage joint from breast plate of bird. Once the plate is removed, the rest of the boning will be easier. You have to tease and work the meat from the plate. Slowly detach the skin from the back, working your way towards the legs.

Detach thighs from backbone by cutting through the joint. Work through by cutting slowly from both sides. Continue to pull skin back over hipbone.

Pull skin over the legs. It should begin to fall off of its own accord. Keep working the skin carefully so that it doesn't tear.

Using kitchen shears, cut through the tailbone and pull skin from backbone.

Using kitchen shears, cut through tailbone and pull skin totally from backbone.

To remove thighbone: Slowly cut meat from thighbone. Cut thighbone through joint and remove. Leave drumstick in place.

Pull off all excess fat from skin. Cut off wing tips.

Cut the thighbone through joint and remove, leaving the drumstick in place.

2.   Prepare lotus seeds: Place lotus seeds in 3 cups water, and bring to a boil. Lower heat, partially cover, and let cook for 2 hours, until tender. Drain and reserve.

3.   Marinate shrimp for 30 minutes. Heat a wok over high heat for 45 seconds; place 1½ tablespoons peanut oil in wok and use a spatula to coat sides. Add minced ginger, stir-fry for 30 seconds, and add shrimp. Spread shrimp in a thin layer. When shrimp start to turn pink, turn over and stir until shrimp completely change color. Remove and set aside.

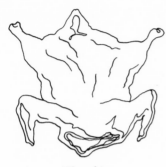

The skin

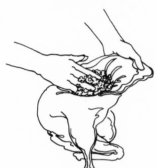

Stuff the duck.

4. Coat duck inside and out with mixture of white vinegar and Shao-Hsing wine or sherry. Sew neck opening of duck closed.

5. Wash and drain glutinous rice 4 times. The last time be certain to drain it thoroughly through a strainer. Place rice in a round cake pan, add 3 cups chicken broth, place in a steamer, and steam (see steaming directions, page 46) for 30 to 45 minutes. When cooked, remove and place rice in a large mixing bowl.

6. Add shrimp, lotus seeds, water chestnuts, mushrooms, scallions, bamboo shoots, oyster sauce, sesame oil, light and dark soy sauces, sugar, minced garlic, and white pepper to the rice. Mix all together by hand until blended thoroughly.

7. Stuff the mixture into duck cavity. Sew the duck closed. Pat duck back to its former shape. Coat with dark soy sauce.

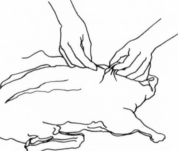

Sew the opening closed.

Roast the duck on a rack.

8. Preheat oven to 450° F. for 20 minutes. Place duck on a rack in a foil-lined roasting pan and place in oven to roast for 1 hour. Turn duck over at the halfway point. The duck should roast to a rich, brown color.

9. Remove from oven. Place on a large serving platter and slice across almost like pâté. Serve immediately.

NOTE: Both the boning and the lotus seed preparation can be done a day earlier. Both duck and lotus seed should be refrigerated and covered.

HOM
SOON
CHOI
CHAU
NGAU YUK

*Beef and Sour
Mustard Pickle*

The Cantonese eat Sour Mustard Pickle with fish, almost exclusively. The Hakka prefer it with pork or beef. The mustard pickle was also suited to their nomadic life because once it had been cured, pickled in brine, it kept for a very long time.

12 ounces London broil: slice across the grain into pieces ½ inch by 2 inches

For a marinade for beef, combine in a bowl and mix well:
  ¾ teaspoon salt
  1 teaspoon sugar
  ½ teaspoon ginger juice mixed with 2 teaspoons
      Shao-Hsing wine or sherry
  1 tablespoon oyster sauce
  1 teaspoon dark soy sauce
  1 teaspoon sesame oil
  1 tablespoon cornstarch
      Pinch of white pepper

4½ tablespoons peanut oil
  1 slice of fresh ginger
  ¼ teaspoon salt
2½ cups sour mustard pickle: separate stalks from leaves; slice stalks diagonally at ½-inch intervals; cut leaves into ½-inch pieces
  2 teaspoons sugar
  5 fresh water chestnuts: peel, wash, dry, slice thinly
  4 ounces snow peas: remove strings and both ends, wash, dry, cut diagonally into ½-inch pieces
  1 tablespoon cloud ears: soak in hot water for 30 minutes, wash, drain off excess water
  2 garlic cloves, minced

To make a sauce, combine in a bowl and mix well:
2 teaspoons cornstarch
2 teaspoons oyster sauce
1 teaspoon dark soy sauce
1 teaspoon sugar
¼ teaspoon salt
1 teaspoon sesame oil
Pinch of white pepper
¼ cup chicken broth

Sprigs of coriander

1. Marinate beef for 30 minutes.

2. Heat a wok over high heat for 45 seconds. Add 2 tablespoons peanut oil and coat wok sides with a spatula. Add slice of ginger and the salt; stir around. When a wisp of white smoke appears, add stalks of mustard pickle; stir for 45 seconds. Add sugar; mix together. Add water chestnuts, snow peas, cloud ears; stir together for 1½ minutes. Add leaves of mustard pickle; stir together. Remove from wok and reserve.

3. Wash and dry wok and spatula. Place back over high heat. Add 2½ tablespoons peanut oil. Coat wok with a spatula. Add minced garlic. When it turns brown, add beef and marinade. Spread meat in a thin layer. Let it cook for 1½ to 2 minutes, turn over, and mix well.

4. Add vegetables; mix together. Make a well in the center, stir sauce, and pour in. Combine all ingredients thoroughly. When sauce thickens and turns brown, remove from wok and serve immediately, garnished with coriander.

NOTE: Occasionally the mustard pickle is overly sour or salty, depending upon the individual curing or pickling time. If too salty or sour, soak it in water for 2 to 3 hours. Taste to see if still too salty. A touch of sugar can be added if needed.

HOK
BOK
TUNG GU

*Black and
White
Mushrooms*

20 dried Chinese black mushrooms, about the size of a
   half-dollar: soak in hot water for 30 minutes,
   wash, remove stems
 2 scallions: wash, dry, discard both ends, cut into 3
   pieces
 1 slice of ginger
 1 teaspoon sugar
 2 teaspoons dark soy sauce
 1 teaspoon sesame oil
½ cup chicken broth
 1 ounce fresh chicken fat

To make a sauce, combine in a bowl and mix well:
1½ tablespoons oyster sauce
 1 teaspoon dark soy sauce
½ teaspoon sugar
 1 teaspoon sesame oil
 1 tablespoon cornstarch
1½ ounces mushroom liquid
   Pinch of white pepper

20 fresh mushrooms, about silver-dollar size: brush
   clean, remove stems
 2 tablespoons peanut oil
 2 teaspoons minced garlic
 2 teaspoons minced ginger
   Sprigs of coriander

1.   Place black mushrooms and scallions, ginger, sugar, dark soy sauce, sesame oil, chicken broth, and chicken fat in a heatproof dish. Mix thoroughly so mushrooms are well coated. Steam over high heat for 20 minutes (see steaming directions, page 46). Remove from heat and allow to cool. Drain off and reserve liquid. Reserve mushrooms. Ginger, scallions, and chicken fat should be discarded.

2.   Make the sauce and reserve it.

3. Water-blanch the fresh mushrooms until water boils (see water blanching directions, page 45). Turn off heat. Run cold water into wok, then drain. Remove mushrooms and reserve them.

4. Heat the wok over high heat for 45 seconds. Add peanut oil; coat wok with a spatula. Add garlic and ginger. When garlic browns, add fresh mushrooms. Stir for 2 minutes. Add black mushrooms; stir-fry for 1½ to 2 minutes, until very hot.

5. Make a well in the center, stir the sauce, pour into the wok, and mix thoroughly. When sauce thickens and turns brown, remove and serve, garnished with coriander.

HAKKA
LIN
BAU
FON

Lotus Leaf Rice,
Hakka-Style

This differs from the vegetarian version of lotus leaf rice, for not only does it contain shrimp and chicken, but it is made with easily obtainable rice instead of the somewhat rarer glutinous rice of the other version. For the Hakka it is a simple enough treat because all one need do is pluck the lotus leaves from ponds that abound in them.

2 lotus leaves
1½ cups extra long-grain rice

Two identical marinades, one for shrimp, one for chicken. For each, combine:
  1 teaspoon ginger juice mixed with 1 teaspoon
      white wine
  1 teaspoon light soy sauce
  2 teaspoons oyster sauce
  ¼ teaspoon salt
  ½ teaspoon sugar
  1 teaspoon cornstarch
  1 tablespoon scallion oil (see page 24)
    Pinch of white pepper

8 ounces shrimp: shell, devein, wash, dry, cut into ½-inch pieces

1½ pounds chicken cutlets: remove fat, gristle, membranes, cut into ½-inch dice

3½ tablespoons peanut oil

3 eggs, beaten

2 teaspoons minced ginger

3 teaspoons minced garlic

⅓ cup dried Chinese black mushrooms: soak in hot water for 30 minutes, wash, remove stems, cut into ¼-inch dice

4 fresh water chestnuts: peel, wash, dry, cut into ¼-inch dice

⅓ cup bamboo shoots, cut into ¼-inch dice

3 scallions: discard both ends, wash, dry, slice finely

1 tablespoon scallion oil (see page 24)

1. Soak lotus leaves in hot water for 30 minutes, until soft. Wash; allow excess water to run off. Set aside.

2. Cook rice (see instructions, page 47).

3. Make marinade and marinate shrimp in one batch and chicken in the other for 30 minutes each.

4. Heat a wok over high heat for 1 minute. Add 1 table-spoon peanut oil and coat wok with a spatula. Pour beaten eggs into wok and scramble. Remove from wok and cut eggs into small pieces. Reserve. Wash wok and spatula.

5. Heat wok again over high heat, add 1 tablespoon pea-nut oil, and coat sides. Add 1 teaspoon minced ginger and 1½ teaspoons minced garlic. When a wisp of white smoke appears, add shrimp and marinade, spread in a thin layer. Cook for 2 to 3 minutes, then turn over; mix until shrimp turn pink. Remove and place in a large mixing bowl. Wash wok and spatula.

6. Heat wok again, add 1½ tablespoons peanut oil, and coat wok again. Add remaining minced ginger and garlic. When a wisp of white smoke appears, add chicken and marinade and spread in a thin layer. Let cook for 4 to 5 minutes; turn over and mix well. When chicken turns white in color, add mushrooms, water chestnuts, and bamboo shoots. Mix together well. Remove and place in the bowl with the shrimp.

7. Add pieces of egg, cooked rice, and scallions to the bowl. Using your hands, mix all ingredients thoroughly. At the last, add scallion oil and mix together thoroughly.

8. Place 1 lotus leaf on top of the other, adjusting them so there are no holes to be seen through. The shiny side of the leaves should be face down on work surface. Place rice mixture in center of leaves and fold front, back, and sides to make a package. Place package, folded side down, in a steamer. Steam over high heat for 45 minutes to 1 hour (see steaming directions, page 46). Remove from steamer and place in a serving dish. Cut a hole in the center of the leaf, scoop out rice mixture with a spoon, and serve.

Place rice mixture in the center of the leaves and fold to make a package.

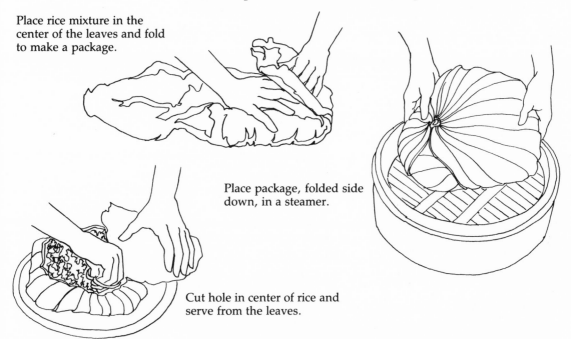

Place package, folded side down, in a steamer.

Cut hole in center of rice and serve from the leaves.

NOTE: This recipe can be prepared in advance, taking all steps up to but not including the steaming process. When ready to prepare and serve, steam the lotus package.

A BANQUET FROM THE SEA

YEUNG GON BUI *Stuffed Scallops*

JAH SAHNG HO *Batter-Fried Oysters*

FAR JIU YIM *Szechuan Peppercorn Salt*

HO JOP SHANGHAI BOK CHOY *Shanghai Bok Choy with Oyster Sauce*

JING LUNG HAR *Steamed Lobster*

DONG GWA HOI SIN TONG *Seafood Wintermelon Soup*

DAU SEE CHAU HAR *Shrimp with Black Beans*

CHAU SAM SIN *Three Seas*

HAI WONG CHAU MEIN *Panfried Noodles with Crab Meat and Chives*

BAK SOI YUE *White Water Fish*

HOI SIN
Food from the Water

There is an expression in Chinese, *hoi sin*, which translates into "ocean fresh," and it is what we say to indicate that the fish or seafood we desire to eat is absolutely fresh. The characters for this expression are exactly the same as those for that wonderful sauce, hoisin, but there is no connection. *Hoi sin*, as it pertains to fish, means that shrimp are alive when you buy them, fish are swimming, crabs and lobsters crawling about. Two of the best places to see an illustration of *hoi sin* are in the Ching Ping Market of Canton and out in Hong Kong's New Territories on a tiny peninsula off Tuen Mun called Mouse Island.

This is not to say that in markets in Hong Kong, Canton, Shanghai, everywhere in China, the fish are anything but fresh, because the Chinese simply wouldn't buy them otherwise, but that in those two wonderful seafood markets every conceivable living thing from the sea is there for your admiration. Ching Ping Market slithers its way through about five blocks of central Canton and amid the fresh fruits and vegetables and the live poultry and fowl are the live fish.

A housewife will bend over a wide galvanized tank and point. A net will be dipped into the tank and the fish placed in another tank with a little water in it, just to wet

179

its gills. The housewife will bend over it, touch it, run her hand along its side. If she is satisfied, it is sold, live, in a plastic bag for her to take home to her family. So it is on Mouse Island. I recall one evening our family went there and bought a "fire-spot bass," shrimp, live crabs, scallops, and oysters. We took them about a mile away to Yung Lung, the Dragon Inn, where they took our bags of seafood and cooked and served it to us. Every taste was so fresh, so keen!

Food from the sea is almost a religion in China, particularly in Canton, Hong Kong, and Shanghai, where it abounds. Every banquet must end with a fish. A fish is a food of honor when presented to a guest. It symbolizes peace, good fortune, wealth. In fact, to the Chinese all seafood has pleasant connotations: Shrimp are happiness, clams good fortune, even seaweed is considered to be good luck because it is the bed from which the fish and shellfish come.

YEUNG
GON
BUI

*Stuffed
Scallops*

I ate this Peking preparation for the first time in the Peking Garden Restaurant in Kowloon, Hong Kong, and the chef was good enough to share it with me.

6 ounces shrimp: shell, devein, wash, dry

For the shrimp stuffing, combine in a bowl:
  ½ teaspoon grated ginger mixed with ½ teaspoon white wine
  2 tablespoons finely sliced scallions, white portions only
  1 teaspoon oyster sauce
  1 teaspoon sesame oil
  2 teaspoons egg white, beaten
  ¼ teaspoon salt
  ½ teaspoon sugar
  1½ teaspoons cornstarch
    Pinch of white pepper

10 large sea scallops, about 1½ inches in diameter, 1 inch thick
  2 teaspoons cornstarch, for dusting
  2 extra large egg whites, beaten with ⅛ teaspoon salt and pinch of white pepper
  ½ cup flour
  5 cups plus 1 tablespoon peanut oil
  1 slice of ginger, ¼ inch thick
  ⅛ teaspoon salt
  8 ounces snow peas: remove strings, discard both ends, wash, dry

1. Place shrimp on a chopping board. Using the cleaver, chop into a paste. Place in the mixing bowl with the stuffing; mix with chopsticks or wooden spoon in one direction until all are blended thoroughly. Refrigerate for 2 hours.

2. Slice scallops into halves through the thickness, creating 2 medallions. Divide shrimp stuffing into 10 equal portions. Sprinkle cornstarch on each half of scallop, then place stuffing on top and the other half of scallop, cornstarch-dusted side down, atop the filling, creating a sandwich. Repeat until 10 are done.

3.   Dip scallops into beaten egg-white mixture until completely coated. Place flour on a large sheet of waxed paper. Roll scallops in flour until well coated. Shake off excess flour and place scallops in a large Chinese strainer.

4.   Heat a wok over high heat for 1 minute; add 5 cups peanut oil. When a wisp of white smoke appears, lower the stuffed scallops into the oil and deep-fry them for 5 minutes, or until scallops turn light brown. Turn off heat, remove scallops from wok, and allow them to drain into a bowl. Wipe wok clean after pouring off the oil.

5.   While scallops are draining, reheat the wok, add 1 tablespoon peanut oil, coat with a spatula, and add ginger and salt. When white smoke appears, add snow peas and stir-fry for 3 to 4 minutes, until snow peas change to a bright green color.

6.   Turn off heat. Place snow peas on a serving dish and spread, making a well in the center. Place scallops in the well and serve immediately.

JAH
SAHNG
HO

*Batter-Fried
Oysters*

Oysters are a favorite all along the coast of China, from Hong Kong to Canton to Shanghai. Cooking them with a batter is the same, whether it be Hong Kong or Shanghai, or points in between.

  5 cups peanut oil
20 medium-size fresh oysters. Have your fish dealer
     open them for you.

To make the batter, mix:

1½ cups high-gluten flour

10 ounces cold water

2 tablespoons baking powder

2 tablespoons peanut oil

1 teaspoon Szechuan Peppercorn Salt (following
    recipe)

1. Heat a wok for 1 minute. Pour in peanut oil. When a
wisp of white smoke appears, cook oysters. Dip each
oyster into the batter until well coated and lower into oil.
Deep-fry five at a time until medium brown, about 3 minutes. Remove oysters and place in a strainer; allow to
drain over a bowl.

2. Deep-fry the last batch to golden brown, about 4 minutes, then place the others back in the oil for about 2 minutes more so they become golden brown as well. Serve all
hot, immediately, with roasted Szechuan peppercorn salt.

FAR
JIU
YIM

*Szechuan
Peppercorn
Salt*

2 teaspoons salt

½ teaspoon 5-spice powder

¼ teaspoon whole Szechuan peppercorns

Heat a wok over medium heat for 45 seconds to 1 minute.
Lower heat and add all ingredients. Dry-roast, stirring occasionally, until 5-spice powder turns black. Remove and
sieve out peppercorns. Put in a small sauce dish and serve
with oysters.

NOTE: This peppercorn salt may also be served with roast
chicken, fried shrimp, and roast duck. It can be made in
advance, but must be kept in a tightly sealed jar. It will
keep indefinitely.

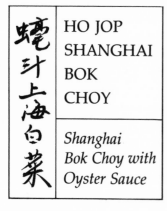

HO JOP SHANGHAI BOK CHOY

Shanghai Bok Choy with Oyster Sauce

This is a very special vegetable, rare in Canton, rare even in Hong Kong. It is a Shanghai product (available widely in the United States) and prepared in a simple manner that emphasizes its distinctive taste.

3 heads of Shanghai Bok Choy, 2½ to 2¾ pounds
6 cups water
½ teaspoon baking soda
1 teaspoon salt
2 tablespoons peanut oil

To make a sauce, combine in a bowl:
2 teaspoons oyster sauce
½ teaspoon dark soy sauce
¼ teaspoon salt
½ teaspoon sugar
½ teaspoon Shao-Hsing wine or sherry
⅛ teaspoon white pepper
2 teaspoons cornstarch
½ cup cold water

1. Remove old, discolored outer leaves of bok choy, trim stems, cut each head lengthwise into quarters. Remove most of leaves. Wash bok choy well under running water to remove sand and dirt. Drain.

2. Heat 6 cups water in a wok; add baking soda and salt. When water boils, add bok choy and bring back to a boil, 3 to 4 minutes. If the process is slow, cover the wok to speed it. Boil for 1 minute; turn off heat. Run cold water into the wok; drain. Run cold water in again; drain. Drain off excess water.

3. Dry wok thoroughly. Place over high heat for 45 seconds. Add 2 tablespoons peanut oil and coat sides of wok with a spatula. When a wisp of white smoke appears, add the bok choy. Stir-fry for 4 minutes, or until hot.

4. Make a well in the center of the wok; stir sauce and pour it in. Stir until sauce thickens. Turn off heat, transfer bok choy to a heated platter, and serve.

JING
LUNG
HAR

*Steamed
Lobster*

This is a most elegant dish from the city of Shanghai. It is almost always served at banquets. It is at once simple to prepare and subtle and rich to serve.

2 fresh-killed raw lobsters, 1¼ pounds each

To make a marinade, combine in a bowl:
   2 tablespoons white wine
   1 tablespoon light soy sauce
   2 tablespoons peanut oil
   1 teaspoon sugar
   ¾ teaspoon salt
   2 teaspoons sesame oil
      Pinch of white pepper
   2 tablespoons shredded ginger

10 thin slices of fresh lemon
 3 scallions, white portions only: thread, cut into 1½-inch lengths
   Sprigs of coriander

1. A fish dealer will kill the lobster for you, split it, devein it, and remove inedible interior portions. Cut head and claws off, cut tail sections into bite-size pieces, and cut claws into pieces. Marinate lobster pieces in the marinade for 30 minutes.

2. In a large oval heatproof dish, arrange the lobster pieces to approximate the original shape. Pour marinade over it. Sprinkle it with lemon slices and scallions and steam in a wok for 20 minutes (see steaming instructions, page 46) until lobster shell turns red. Serve immediately, garnished with sprigs of coriander.

NOTE: It is suggested that this be eaten with some plain rice to take advantage of the delicious sauce.

**DONG GWA
HOI SIN
TONG**

*Seafood
Wintermelon
Soup*

Wintermelon has the special quality of taking on the tastes of what it is cooked with. I have adapted a traditional soup, usually made with pork or chicken, into one that should please shrimp and crab meat fanciers.

4 ounces shrimp: shell, devein, wash, dry, cut into ½-inch pieces

For marinade for shrimp, combine in a bowl:
   ½ teaspoon salt
   1 teaspoon sugar
1½ teaspoons oyster sauce
   1 teaspoon sesame oil
      Pinch of white pepper
   ¼ teaspoon white wine

   2 tablespoons peanut oil
   1 slice of ginger
   ½ teaspoon salt
2½ pounds wintermelon: peel, seed, cut into ½-inch dice
4½ cups fish broth (see page 49)
3½ cups water
   6 dried Chinese black mushrooms: soak in hot water for 30 minutes; wash, remove stems, cut into ½-inch dice
   ¼ cup green peas
   ½ cup crab meat
   1 tablespoon scallion oil (see page 24)
   1 teaspoon sesame oil
   2 egg whites, beaten

1.   Marinate shrimp for 30 minutes. Reserve.

2.   Heat a wok over high heat for 45 seconds. Add peanut oil, ginger, and salt.

3.   Using a spatula, coat the wok with the oil. When a wisp of white smoke appears, add melon and stir-fry for 1 to 2 minutes.

4. Transfer melon to a large pot; add seafood broth, water, and mushrooms. Cover and bring to a boil. Lower heat and cook for 3 to 5 minutes.

5. When melon is tender, raise heat to high, add peas, and bring to a boil. Add shrimp and marinade and crab meat and bring back to a boil. Add scallion oil and sesame oil and stir in. Add beaten egg whites and gently stir into soup. Turn off heat. Pour into a preheated tureen and serve immediately.

NOTE: This soup can be made ahead, but if you do so, add ½ teaspoon baking soda along with the seafood broth and water. This preserves the bright color of the melon.

DAU
SEE
CHAU
HAR

Shrimp with Black Beans

This Cantonese dish is almost a signature of the province. Mention the preparation to a Chinese and he will think, and say: Canton.

  4 tablespoons black beans: wash three times and drain
  4 to 6 garlic cloves
1½ pounds shrimp: shell, devein, wash, and dry

To make a marinade, combine in a bowl and mix well:
  1 tablespoon white wine mixed with 1 teaspoon
       ginger juice
1½ tablespoons oyster sauce
  2 teaspoons light soy sauce
  1 teaspoon sesame oil
  ½ to 1 teaspoon salt
  1 teaspoon sugar
  3 teaspoons cornstarch
    Pinch of white pepper

3½ tablespoons peanut oil
 ½ cup cold water (reserve for final cooking)

1.   Mash together the black beans and the garlic to make a paste. Reserve. Marinate the shrimp; allow to stand for 30 minutes to 1 hour.

2.   In a wok heat the peanut oil over high heat until white smoke appears. Add the bean and garlic paste, break up with a spatula and cook until garlic turns brown. Drain shrimp, reserving the marinade, and place in the wok, separating them into a single layer. Tip wok from side to side to assure even cooking, then turn shrimp over and stir together with paste.

3.   As the shrimp are cooking, add the marinade to the wok and continue to stir-fry. There should be enough moisture to cook properly. If not, add a little of the reserved water. When shrimp turn pink and curl up, they are ready. Turn off heat, remove from wok, and serve immediately.

NOTE: A bit of color in the presentation can be added by garnishing the shrimp with sprigs of coriander.

CHAU SAM SIN	
Three Seas	

8 ounces shrimp: shell, devein, wash, dry
8 ounces uncooked lobster tail: remove meat from shell and devein, slice lengthwise, then cut into ½-inch pieces

Two identical marinades, one for shrimp, one for lobster. For each, combine:
   ½ teaspoon ginger juice mixed with 1 teaspoon white wine
   ¼ teaspoon salt
   1½ teaspoons oyster sauce
   1 teaspoon light soy sauce
   1 teaspoon sesame oil
   ¾ teaspoon sugar
   ¾ teaspoon cornstarch
      Pinch of white pepper

5½ tablespoons peanut oil
  2 slices of fresh ginger
  1 cup fresh asparagus, tip halves only: remove scales,
      wash, dry, cut diagonally at ¼-inch intervals
  ½ cup bamboo shoots: cut into pieces ½ inch by 1½
      inches
  8 fresh water chestnuts: peel, wash, dry, slice thinly
  8 scallions, white portions only: slice lengthwise into
      quarters, then into 1½-inch pieces
  2 garlic cloves, minced
  8 ounces crab meat, picked over
  1 tablespoon cornstarch mixed with 7 tablespoons fish
      broth (see page 49)

1.   Marinate shrimp and lobster separately for 30 minutes. Reserve.

2.   Heat a wok over high heat, add 2 tablespoons peanut oil, coat the wok with a spatula, and add 1 slice of ginger. When a wisp of white smoke appears, add asparagus and bamboo shoots; stir-fry together for 45 seconds. Add water chestnuts, mix, and stir-fry for another minute. Add scallions, mix, and stir-fry for another minute. Remove vegetables from wok and reserve them. Wash wok and spatula.

3.   Heat the wok again over high heat. Add 3½ tablespoons peanut oil and coat the wok. Add the other slice of ginger and 2 minced garlic cloves. When garlic browns, add shrimp and lobster, and spread them in a thin layer. Cook for 1½ minutes and turn over. Shrimp will become pink, lobster white. Then add crab meat and mix 3 seafoods together for 1 minute. Add vegetables and combine well.

4.   Make a well in the center of the mixture, add the cornstarch and seafood-broth mixture, and stir thoroughly until sauce thickens, 1 to 2 minutes. Before removing from wok, taste to see if the cornstarch is completely cooked and blended. Serve immediately.

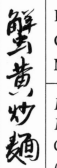

HAI WONG CHAU MEIN

Panfried Noodles with Crab Meat and Chives

Once again I have adapted a traditional recipe, a preparation with its roots in Shanghai that is usually prepared with meat, to take advantage of the subtle taste of crab meat. I have also used a thinner noodle than usual to create a different texture.

8 ounces fresh egg noodles, thin Cantonese style
1 teaspoon salt
1¼ cups yellow chives or threaded scallions: use white portions and tender parts of the green
4½ tablespoons peanut oil
1 tablespoon minced ginger
1¼ teaspoons minced garlic
6 ounces crab meat, picked over

To make a sauce, combine in a bowl and mix well:
¼ teaspoon salt
¼ teaspoon sugar
½ teaspoon dark soy sauce
3½ teaspoons oyster sauce
1½ teaspoons sesame oil
1½ tablespoons cornstarch
1 cup fish broth (see page 49)
Pinch of white pepper

1. Cook noodles in 6 cups of boiling water, with 1 teaspoon salt, for 10 seconds. Add cold water to noodles, then drain. Refill pot with cold water and drain again. Repeat once more, for a total of three times. Place noodles in a strainer to drain thoroughly, for 1 to 1½ hours. Turn occasionally.

2. Wash and dry yellow chives or scallions and cut into 1½-inch lengths. If scallions are used, quarter the white portions. Set aside.

3. In a large cast-iron frying pan heat 3 tablespoons of peanut oil over high heat. When a wisp of white smoke appears, place noodles in the pan and spread evenly.

Cook over high heat for 1 minute, then lower heat and move pan around the burner to allow the edges to cook evenly. Cook for about 10 minutes until noodles are light brown. If noodles stick to pan, add a little more oil. Turn noodles over and repeat.

4. Heat a wok over high heat and add 1½ tablespoons peanut oil. Using a spatula, coat the wok, then add ginger and garlic. When garlic turns light brown, add the crab meat. Toss for 1½ to 2 minutes, until crab meat is hot. Add chives or scallions and mix.

5. Make a well in the center of the mixture, stir the sauce, and pour it into the well. Stir thoroughly. When the mixture thickens and turns brown, turn off heat.

6. Place noodles on a preheated serving dish, pour crab-meat and chive mixture on top, and serve immediately.

BAK
SOI
YUE

*White Water
Fish*

This is called white water, as were the shrimp, because it is cooked, or poached, in boiling, bubbling, "white" water. This preparation is native to Suzhou, near Shanghai. There, a fish called *Ching Yue,* or a toothed green fish like a carp, is used. There are of course no green fish here, so I make this Suzhou dish with sea bass.

3 quarts cold water

"White Water" ingredients
4 fresh bay leaves
6 fresh mint leaves
2 garlic cloves, whole and peeled
3 scallions: wash, discard ends, cut into 3 pieces
3 tablespoons peanut oil
2 teaspoons salt
3 teaspoons sugar

1 whole sea bass, 1½ to 1¾ pounds: clean and wash
    well, remove all membranes, dry thoroughly
3 tablespoons peanut oil
2 tablespoons shredded ginger
2 scallions: wash, dry, discard all green portions, shred
    white portions into 1½-inch pieces

To make the sauce, combine in a bowl:
2½ tablespoons light soy sauce
1 teaspoon sugar
1 teaspoon white wine
1 teaspoon white vinegar
    Pinch of white pepper

1 teaspoon sesame oil

1.   In an oval Dutch oven bring 3 quarts water to a boil and add all "White Water" ingredients. Boil over high heat for 4 to 5 minutes. Place the fish in the liquid, cover, and turn off heat. Let fish sit for 10 minutes. Remove fish, place in a serving dish, and discard the other ingredients.

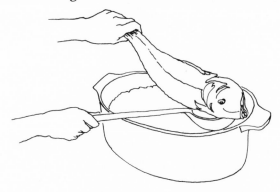

2.   Heat a wok over high heat and add peanut oil. When a wisp of white smoke appears, add ginger and scallions. Stir briefly, then add sauce. Bring to a boil. Turn heat off, add sesame oil, mix well, and pour contents of wok over fish. Serve immediately.

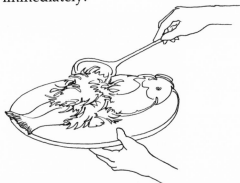

NOTE: In China this dish is cooked in a wok. The wok cover is made of wood, 1½ inches thick. It seals the heat in better than a thick, cast-iron cover. These wood covers are unavailable here, therefore a Dutch oven or a fish poacher is a fine substitute.

A VEGETARIAN BANQUET

JAI HO SEE · *Vegetarian Oysters*

JAI SIU NGAW · *Vegetarian Goose*

CHAU JAI MAI FUN · *Spicy Rice Noodles*

CHING CHAU YAU CHOI · *Stir-Fried Choi Sum*

BOH DOH DONG GUA JUNG · *Steamed Whole Wintermelon Soup*

CHUNG JIN DAO FU · *Bean Curd Panfried with Scallions*

JAI WOO LO YUK · *Vegetarian Sweet and Sour Pork*

LIN BAU NOR MAI FAN · *Vegetarian Stuffed Lotus Leaves*

JAI YUE · *Vegetarian Fish*

CHOY
Food from the Earth

My first memories of vegetarianism as an observance rest with my grandmother. I recall, as a little girl, that every month on the first and the fifteenth, and every January for the first fifteen days of the month, my grandmother would eat no meat. At other times she would eat pork or poultry and some fish. On those days she would sit in a corner of her salon and pray, fingering her beads as she did so. When I asked her about this she told me she was observing the laws of Buddha. She was not a strict vegetarian, as you can see, but she fasted according to her beliefs. Those beliefs also extended to her absolute abstinence from beef because it was forbidden by Buddha.

The tradition of eating only vegetables has its roots in Buddhism and in Taoism. Buddhist monks will never eat meat; Taoists will, if they desire, but few do. As happens so often with beliefs, eating vegetables became a sometime tradition in China, but as the tradition spread so did interpretations of it.

If you couldn't have meat, why not deceive yourself into thinking you have meat by creating "meat" from vegetables? Why not create "fish" as well? And so another tradition was born, one of culinary artifice. I have seen it in many places, in the Ching Chun Koon Taoist monastery in Hong Kong's New Territories, in the Po Lin Buddhist monastery on Lantau Island between Hong Kong and Macao, in the Soh Chun Jai Restaurant (Spring Vegetables), in Hangzhou close by the beautiful West Lake. I have seen "fish" made from taro root and bean curd, vegetarian "bird's nest," "sausages," "beef," and "poultry." These "false" foods, which are to be admired, are artful combinations of vegetables.

What I have tried to do in this section of my book is give a taste of both the creation of *faux* foods and the delicious combinations possible using only vegetables.

齋燒鼓	JAI HO SEE
	Vegetarian Oysters

This is a recipe I learned at the Taoist monastery, Ching Chung Koon, in Hong Kong. In vegetarian cookery, practiced best these days in Buddhist and Taoist temples, the idea is to deceive deliciously. In this case the "oyster" should *look* like an oyster but should surprise and delight the tongue with a wholly different taste.

2 small Chinese eggplants: wash, dry, discard first slice

Batter
1½ cups high-gluten flour
 2 teaspoons baking powder
10 ounces cold water
 2 tablespoons peanut oil

3 tablespoons ginger pickle, shredded (see page 72)
¼ medium onion, sliced thinly
4 cups peanut oil

1. To prepare the eggplants: Slice diagonally at ⅛-inch intervals. Cut the first slice all the way through, then the next about three quarters of the way through, then cut all the way through, to create sandwich pockets. Continue to slice in this manner until all of the eggplant is used. There should be 20 pockets.

2. Make the batter: Place the flour in a bowl; add baking powder, then add water gradually, stirring until smooth. Add peanut oil and blend in until batter is even and smooth. Set aside.

3. In each eggplant pocket put 5 to 6 pieces of shredded ginger pickle and an equal amount of sliced onion. Repeat until all eggplant pockets are filled.

4. In a wok, heat the peanut oil to 350° F. Dip each "oyster" into the batter, holding tightly with chopsticks or tongs. Coat well and place in the oil, 4 or 5 "oysters" at a time.

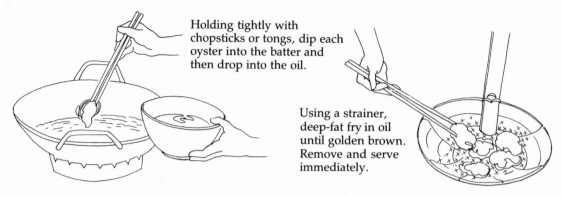

Holding tightly with chopsticks or tongs, dip each oyster into the batter and then drop into the oil.

Using a strainer, deep-fat fry in oil until golden brown. Remove and serve immediately.

5. As soon as you place "oysters" in oil, turn off heat. When they brown on one side, turn over. Turn heat on again to bring temperature up. Oil should be a constant 325° to 350° F., no higher, so that eggplant pockets are fried to a golden brown color. Remove and serve immediately.

JAI
SIU
NGAW

Vegetarian Goose

In any Chinese banquet it is virtually obligatory to have fish, fowl, and meat. It is just as important in a vegetarian version to imitate these courses. So, with vegetarian goose what you have is bean curd skins cooked so they resemble the skin of a roast goose in both texture and color. Again a triumph of delightful deception.

  1 tablespoon peanut oil, for stir-frying
  ½ cup dried Chinese black mushrooms, 8 to 10: soak in hot water for 30 minutes, wash, remove stems, cut caps into julienne
  ½ cup bamboo shoots: cut into julienne
  ½ cup carrots: cut into julienne

   To make the sauce, combine in a bowl:
    4 teaspoons sesame oil
    4 teaspoons dark soy sauce
    3 teaspoons sugar
     Pinch of white pepper

¼ cup cold water
1 large piece of dry bean-curd skin
4 tablespoons peanut oil, for panfrying
1 cup shredded lettuce

1. In a wok, heat 1 tablespoon peanut oil until a wisp of white smoke appears. Add vegetables and stir-fry briskly. Stir the sauce, add to the wok, and mix. Add water and continue to stir-fry, stirring constantly, until the water evaporates, about 3 minutes. When vegetables are cooked, place them in a dish and set aside.

2. Spread out the bean-curd skin flat on a table or work surface. Using kitchen scissors, cut the skin into 3 sections, 6 by 4 inches. Dip your fingers in water and wet the skin lightly. Make a ridge of vegetables across the long end of the skin sections, roll up, and press closed. If your steamer is small, simply make the rolls to the appropriate size.

3. To steam: Oil a metal pie pan or tempered dish lightly. Place the rolls in the pan or dish and sprinkle the rolls with a tablespoon of water. Place the pan or dish in the steamer. Pour about 4 cups water into a wok and bring to a boil. Place the steamer over the wok and steam for 10 to 15 minutes.

4. Rolls must then be panfried. Pour 4 tablespoons of peanut oil into a pan. Panfry rolls briskly.

5. Cut the rolls into smaller pieces, 4 pieces from each of the 3 rolls made. Arrange them on a bed of lettuce on a platter and serve hot.

Using kitchen scissors, cut the bean-curd skin into sections, 6 inches by 4 inches.

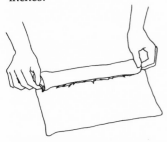

Make a ridge of vegetables across the long end and roll up.

NOTE: The vegetable filling in this recipe makes a delicious mixed vegetable dish to serve with rice.

Bean-curd skin can be purchased in any Asian market. Make sure the skin is fresh. If it is too hard, it is probably stale, and too old to use.

CHAU
JAI
MAI
FUN

*Spicy Rice
Noodles*

6 ounces dry rice noodles (usually sold in 1-pound
    packages, labeled Rice Noodles or Rice Vermicelli)
6 cups water
3½ tablespoons peanut oil
1 tablespoon minced ginger
1 teaspoon salt
3 tablespoons Szechuan mustard pickle, cut into
    julienne
1 large hot red pepper, minced
¾ cup sweet red pepper, cut into julienne
½ cup snow peas: string, remove both ends, cut
    diagonally into julienne
3 scallions: remove both ends, wash, dry, cut into
    julienne
1 teaspoon sesame oil

1.   At least 2½ hours before assembling the dish, boil
noodles in 6 cups water for about 1 minute, separating
noodles as they boil, until they are barely *al dente*. Run
cold water into the pot and drain through a strainer. Add
cold water again and drain. Add cold water once again
and drain. Reserve. During this period separate and turn
noodles three times to ensure that all water has drained.

2.   Heat a wok over high heat for 40 seconds. Add 1½
tablespoons peanut oil; coat the wok with a spatula. Add
minced ginger and ½ teaspoon salt. Cook until ginger
turns light brown. Add all vegetables. Stir-fry for about 1½
minutes, until vegetables are slightly softened. Remove
and drain over a strainer. Reserve.

3.   Wash and dry the wok; place back on heat for 1 minute. Add 2 tablespoons peanut oil and coat the wok. Add
remaining ½ teaspoon salt and wait until wok becomes
quite hot and smoky. Add rice noodles to the wok by allowing them to slide over the spatula into the wok,
thereby avoiding having the noodles splatter into the hot
oil. Separate them as they fry, turning with spatula and
chopsticks.

4. If noodles seem to stick or burn, add an additional 1 tablespoon peanut oil, but *only* if needed. Lower heat and stir-fry until noodles are hot, about 5 minutes. Raise heat and add vegetables. Stir together until mixed thoroughly and hot. Add sesame oil and toss to give the dish a nutty aroma. Turn off heat and transfer noodles to a serving dish.

CHING
CHAU
YAU
CHOI

*Stir-Fried
Choi Sum*

Choi sum is one of the most delicious of Chinese vegetables. It is bright green, resembling Chinese broccoli, but has small, yellow, budlike flowers, and is available in Chinese vegetable markets. When cooked, it is very sweet. From the time I was a little girl I can always remember loving the vegetable for its sweetness and wanting it by itself without any additional flavors or ingredients.

2 bunches of choi sum
1 slice of fresh ginger, ¼ inch thick
8 cups cold water
½ teaspoon baking soda
2½ tablespoons peanut oil
¼ teaspoon salt

1. Wash choi sum. Break off tender top portions, about 4 to 5 inches. Discard the large leaves and flowers. Set aside.

2. In a large pot place the ginger, water, and baking soda and bring to a boil. Add choi sum and water-blanch for 1 to 2 minutes, until it becomes bright green (see water-blanching directions, page 45). Turn off heat, remove pot from stove, and pour through a strainer. Run under cold water for 1 minute, then set aside. Choi sum must be thoroughly drained, so allow to sit for 1 to 1½ hours.

3. Heat a wok over high heat. Add peanut oil and spread with a spatula to coat wok. Add salt and stir. When white smoke appears, add choi sum. Stir-fry for 2 to 3 minutes, until hot. Place in a dish and serve immediately.

NOTE: The discarded portions of choi sum may be used as soup ingredients.

BOH DOH
DONG
GUA
JUNG

*Steamed Whole
Wintermelon
Soup*

What makes this such an unusual preparation is that the melon itself becomes the cooking pot and the serving tureen for the soup that is brewed in it. No feast in either a Buddhist or a Taoist temple would be complete without this soup.

   3 cups water
½ cup peanuts
   1 wintermelon, 10 pounds
⅓ cup gingko nuts (see note)
⅓ cup fresh mushrooms: brush clean, discard stems, cut into ½-inch dice
½ cup straw mushrooms: cut into quarters
½ cup dried Chinese black mushrooms: soak until softened, wash, discard stems, cut caps into ½-inch dice
½ cup carrots: peel, wash, cut into ½-inch dice
½ cup bamboo shoots: cut into ½-inch dice
⅓ cup water chestnuts: peel, wash, dry, cut into ½-inch dice
½ cup green peas, fresh or frozen
1½ teaspoons minced ginger
   1 teaspoon minced garlic
   2 tablespoons scallion oil (see page 24)
5½ cups vegetable broth (see page 49)

   Special tools
   A large pot, such as a lobster pot

1.   In a pot bring 3 cups of water to a boil. Add peanuts and simmer for 1 hour. Drain and set aside.

2.   Place the wintermelon in its cook pot, *for measurement purposes only*, in this manner: Put a cake rack on the bottom of the pot; place melon on it. You will need a very large pot, such as a lobster pot. With a pencil mark the melon where it is even with the top of the pot. Remove melon and cake rack from pot. Cut melon straight across top at measurement line. Discard top.

Create a serrated edge
around the rim of the melon.

Place melon on rack and
secure with strings.

3. Using a grapefruit knife or similar tool remove seeds and pulp of melon. Create a serrated edge around the rim of the melon. Place nuts, vegetables, and oil inside melon cavity. Pour in vegetable broth. Set melon aside.

4. Put 2 to 3 inches of water in the cooking pot. As the water comes to a boil, prepare the melon: Tie 6 lengths of string to the rim of the cake rack. Place melon on the rack. Bring strings up over to the open top end and join together in one knot over center of the opening. The strings should be pulled tight to secure the melon.

5. Lift the melon by means of the knot and lower it into the boiling water. Cover pot and steam for at least 1 hour. Depending upon the age and size of the melon, cooking time will vary from 1 to 1½ hours. After the first hour, check every 8 or 10 minutes to see if the melon is tender. Do not overcook or the outer skin of the melon will begin to sag. The melon and the soup are done when the inside of the melon is tender.

6. To serve, lift the melon and rack from pot and place on an attractive plate. Cut strings and remove them. Ladle the soup into bowls, then carefully shave pieces of melon from the inside and place 1 or 2 pieces into each bowl.

NOTE: Gingko nuts are usually available in Chinese grocery stores, either fresh or canned. They have a beautiful yellow color and add tremendously to the beauty of the soup. They are also delicious. If you use fresh gingkos, which I prefer, follow this procedure:

Put 3 cups water in a pot and bring to a boil. Crack 1 cup gingko nuts, discard the shells, and place nuts in the boiling water. Bring water back to a boil, reduce heat, and allow nuts to cook for 20 minutes. Turn off heat, run cold water in the pot, then pour it off. Skin the nuts and reserve them for the soup. This will yield ⅓ cup of skinned nuts.

If fresh nuts are unavailable, used canned gingkos. If they are not available, substitute chestnuts.

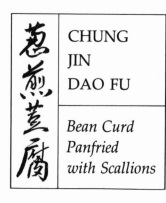

CHUNG
JIN
DAO FU

*Bean Curd
Panfried
with Scallions*

4½ tablespoons peanut oil
6 cakes of fresh bean curd: dry thoroughly with paper
     towels
¼ teaspoon salt
8 to 10 scallions: wash, dry, cut off both ends, cut into
     1½-inch pieces (NOTE: Often white portions are
     thick and should be quartered.)

To make a sauce, combine in bowl and mix well:
   2 tablespoons dark soy sauce
   1½ tablespoons cornstarch
   ¼ teaspoon salt
   1 teaspoon sugar
   1 cup vegetable broth or cold water

1. In a flat-bottomed, cast-iron frying pan heat 3 table-spoons of peanut oil. When white smoke appears, place bean curd cakes in the pan and fry for 5 to 7 minutes, until they turn light brown. If heat is too high, lower it. Turn cakes over and repeat. Remove cakes from pan, place in a serving dish, and cut into 1-inch pieces.

2. Heat a wok over high heat. Add remainder of peanut oil and the salt. Coat wok sides with a spatula. When white smoke appears, add white portions of scallions; stir-fry for 30 seconds. Add green portions; stir-fry until they become bright green. Remove scallions from wok and reserve.

3. Stir sauce ingredients and pour into wok over low heat. Stir clockwise continuously until sauce thickens and becomes dark brown. Add scallions and mix well. Turn off heat, pour contents of wok over bean curd pieces, and serve.

NOTE: For those who prefer not to fry the bean curd, it can be steamed (see directions, page 46), then served in the same way.

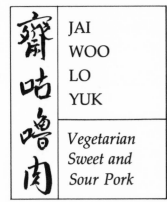

JAI
WOO
LO
YUK

*Vegetarian
Sweet and
Sour Pork*

Here again, the idea is to have you see and think of a familiar dish, in this case the sweet and sour pork of Peking and Canton. When you see the "pork" put in front of you, your thoughts are of pork; when you bite into the first morsel, you discover the pork is a walnut.

40 whole walnuts, halved

Batter ingredients
1½ cups high-gluten flour
  2 teaspoons baking powder
10 ounces cold water
  2 tablespoons peanut oil

4 to 5 cups peanut oil

To make the sauce, combine in a saucepan and set aside:
  9 tablespoons red-wine vinegar
  9 tablespoons sugar
  6 tablespoons tomato sauce
  2 tablespoons cornstarch mixed with 2 tablespoons
      cold water
  2 teaspoons dark soy sauce
¾ cup cold water

½ cup sweet red pepper: wash, dry, cut into ¾-inch
    cubes
½ cup fresh green pepper: wash, dry, cut into ¾-inch
    cubes
¼ cup carrots: peel, wash, cut into pieces ⅛ by ¾ inch
½ cup canned pineapple: cut into ¾-inch cubes

1. Cook walnuts: Heat 4 cups water to boiling. Place walnuts in boiling water for 5 minutes to remove bitter taste. Remove from water, drain, and run cold water over them. Drain again, then place back in the wok with another 4 cups water. Bring to a boil, cook for another 5 minutes, and repeat draining process. Set aside and let drain until completely dry.

2. To make the batter, place flour in a bowl, add baking powder, and mix together. Add water slowly with one hand while stirring it into flour with chopsticks. Add peanut oil and blend thoroughly until batter is smooth. Set aside.

3. Place a wok over high heat for 45 seconds to 1 minute. Add peanut oil. When white smoke appears, place a flat strainer holding the walnuts into the oil. Deep-fry for about 5 minutes; remove and set aside to cool.

4. Strain peanut oil from wok to remove any walnut particles. Return oil to wok over high heat and heat oil to 350°F. Using chopsticks or tongs, dip walnuts into batter and place in oil. Cook for 2 to 3 minutes on each side, until golden brown. Cook 4 or 5 walnuts at one time. Repeat until all walnuts are fried. Place in a serving dish.

5. Over medium heat, heat the sauce, stirring constantly. When sauce starts to darken and thicken and begins to bubble, add vegetables and pineapple, stir together, and mix until sauce begins to bubble again. Pour the mixture into a sauceboat and serve with the "pork."

LIN BAU
NOR MAI
FAN

*Vegetarian
Stuffed
Lotus Leaves*

The concept of steaming glutinous rice and other ingredients in lotus leaf wrappings is Cantonese, and I can recall my father using that technique to create many variations of the stuffed lotus leaf. This is my version of one of my father's recipes.

10 cups cold water
¾ cup peeled raw chestnuts
½ cup skinned raw peanuts
2 cups glutinous rice: wash 3 times, drain
2 large lotus leaves
½ cup straw mushrooms: cut into ¼-inch pieces
½ cup fresh mushrooms: cut into ¼-inch pieces
½ cup bamboo shoots: cut into ¼-inch pieces
3 fresh water chestnuts: peel, wash, dry, cut into ¼-inch pieces

3 scallions: discard both ends, wash, dry, cut into ⅛-
    inch pieces
1 teaspoon salt
2 teaspoons sugar
1½ teaspoons light soy sauce
1½ teaspoons dark soy sauce
2 teaspoons sesame oil
2 tablespoons scallion oil (see page 24)
  Pinch of white pepper

1. Place 4 cups cold water in pot. Add chestnuts, bring water to a boil, lower heat, partially cover, and cook for 1 hour, until chestnuts are tender. Allow to cool, then cut into ½-inch pieces. Reserve.

2. Repeat the process with the peanuts, but do not cut them up. Reserve.

3. Place drained rice in a cake pan, add 2 cups cold water, and steam for 30 to 40 minutes (see steaming directions, page 46). Reserve.

4. While rice is cooking, soak lotus leaves in hot water for 30 minutes. Then wash, and reserve.

5. When rice is cooked, place in a large bowl and add all ingredients except lotus leaves. Mix thoroughly with hands. Place 1 lotus leaf atop the other, positioning them so no holes can be seen. Mound the rice and other ingredients on the leaves.

6. Make a package by folding the leaves to cover the rice on all four sides. Place the package folded side down on a steamer and steam for 45 minutes to 1 hour, until hot, to allow the flavors of all ingredients to blend.

7. Remove package from steamer onto a dish. Cut a round hole in the top of the package and serve.

NOTE: Bamboo leaves may be substituted for lotus leaves. The preparation may be made 1 day in advance. Keep refrigerated, then allow to come to room temperature before steaming.

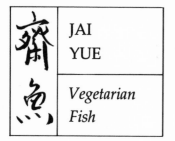

JAI
YUE

*Vegetarian
Fish*

Once again the intent is to make the mind go in one direction, the palate in another. This *looks* like a fish, but the tastes and textures are entirely vegetable. It is a wonderful deception, one practiced both in Hong Kong and in several of the finer vegetarian restaurants in Hangzhou.

    1 to 1¼ pounds uncooked taro root
    ½ teaspoon salt
    1 teaspoon sugar
      Pinch of white pepper
    1 cup plain bread crumbs
    ½ cup wheat starch
    ⅞ cup boiling water
    6 tablespoons peanut oil
    ⅓ cup sliced almonds
    1 black olive
    5 cups peanut oil
      Sprigs of parsley

1. Cut taro root into quarters, or 2-inch-thick slices, and place in a steamer. Add 4 to 5 cups water to a wok, bring to a boil, and place steamer over water (see steaming directions, page 46). Cook for 1 to 1½ hours. Keep additional water on hand to replace that which evaporates. To test taro: Insert a chopstick into a piece of root; if it goes in easily, the taro is cooked. Remove from wok and allow to cool.

2. Peel skin off taro root and discard it. Mash root by hand and discard any hard pieces (which will not cook properly). There should be 2½ cups mashed root. Place mashed root in a large bowl and add salt, sugar, white pepper, and bread crumbs; mix together.

3. Make a wheat-starch paste: Place wheat starch in a bowl and add ⅞ cup boiling water, stirring constantly with chopsticks or a wooden spoon until mixture thickens. Add to taro mixture and blend.

4. Add 6 tablespoons peanut oil to mixture and knead until a dough is formed. If dough is dry, add 1 to 2 more tablespoons of peanut oil. Refrigerate, uncovered, for 4 hours, or covered, overnight.

5. Form a fish: Place dough on a large sheet of wax paper. Mold into a fish shape, adding sliced almonds as scales, working from the tail end to the front. Cut the olive into an eye shape and place on fish's head. Use a pizza cutter or a fork to make fin lines on tail and fins.

6. Heat a wok for 45 seconds to 1 minute, then add 5 cups peanut oil. Heat to 350° F. Put fish into the oil by means of a flat strainer and cook for 5 to 7 minutes, until brown. Serve immediately, garnished with sprigs of parsley.

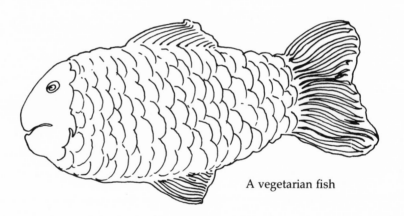

A vegetarian fish

A BANQUET FOR THE NEW YEAR

SEE JOP CHAU HIN	*Clams with Black Beans*
FAT CHOI JAI	*Buddha's Delight*
YOK FAR BUN LOP CHEUNG	*Broccoli and Lop Cheung*
SAH DEH NGAU YUK	*Beef Saté*
YUE CHI TONG	*Shark's-Fin Soup*
CHOI PEI NOR MAI GAI	*Kwangtung Crispy Stuffed Chicken*
SEE SIU JUE BEI	*Soy Sauce Roast Ham*
YANGZHOU CHAU FAN	*Fried Rice Yangzhou Style*
CHOY PEI SEK BON	*Crispy Sea Bass*

GUNG HAY FAT CHOY

新年家宴主席

Cooking for a Happy New Year

The New Year holiday is the happiest day of the year for the Chinese. It is the day when everything begins anew. On this first day of the first month of the lunar calendar, whatever we did was supposed to suggest newness, freshness, a beginning, regeneration, and of course long life and good fortune. On the seventh day of the New Year it was *yan yat*, everybody's birthday. We began looking forward to it at the beginning of our twelfth month, counting the days until we would get our "lucky money" from our elders, when we would be able to eat unlimited amounts of sugar cane and sweet dumplings shaped like ancient gold coins, called *taels*, as well as slices of sweet sugar-and-rice cakes.

On New Year's Day Buddhists, like my grandmother, would eat only vegetables, and this is one of the reasons that she would not come to our house on that day. My mother, a modern woman, observed the New Year in her own way. She would not prepare a vegetarian meal, but would have at least one vegetables-only dish. And she would observe in other ways.

There would always be a clam preparation of some kind because clams symbolize good fortune. She would hang a scallion over our doorway as a symbol of spring and cook scallions because they were hollow and represented wisdom. There would be oranges and tangerines and things prepared with honey, all of which said to us and our guests that there would be sweetness in our lives. There would be pork, a symbol of plenty, and *lop cheung* sausages, because their lengths reminded us of longevity. As you can see, our house had a feast on New Year's Day, a banquet that was full of symbolism, including obeisances to Buddha, but was not narrow or limiting, simply because that was the way my mother was.

What I have tried to do is prepare the same sort of traditional New Year banquet. There is a vegetable dish; there are clams, scallions, honey, pork, and *lop cheung*, among other things. It is quite close to what my mother would have come up with, and I think she would have liked it.

SEE
JOP
CHAU
HIN

Clams with Black Beans

Like virtually all of the dishes on New Year's Day, clams are symbolic. They represent prosperity; in particular, when the clams open after cooking, they vaguely resemble taels, the gold coins of past ages.

30 medium-size clams: wash with a thick brush to remove dirt and sand
3 tablespoons peanut oil
1 tablespoon shredded ginger
1 tablespoon shredded garlic
2 tablespoons fermented black beans: wash twice, allow excess water to drain off, set aside

To make the sauce, combine:
1½ tablespoons oyster sauce
1 teaspoon dark soy sauce
1 teaspoon sesame oil
¾ teaspoon sugar
1 tablespoon cornstarch
Pinch of white pepper
5 ounces chicken broth

2 tablespoons finely shredded scallions, white portions only

1.   Pour 8 cups water into a wok and bring to a boil. Place clams in the wok and bring water back to a boil; this should take 4 to 5 minutes. Clams will begin to open. Move them around with your spatula to help the process. As they open remove them to a waiting dish, or they will toughen. Continue until all are open. Set them aside. Discard water; wash wok and spatula.

2.   Heat the wok over high heat for 40 seconds. Add peanut oil and use a spatula to coat the wok with oil. Add ginger, garlic, and black beans. Stir until garlic browns. Add clams; stir and mix for 2 minutes.

3. Make a well in the center; stir the sauce and pour it in. Stir thoroughly and continually until sauce thickens; make sure all clams are thoroughly coated with sauce.

4. Turn off heat, place clams and sauce in a serving dish, sprinkle scallions on top of them, and serve immediately.

FAT
CHOI
JAI

*Buddha's
Delight*

Another must dish for a New Year's banquet, because it is an observance as well as something wonderful to eat. It is a celebration of Buddhist vegetarianism and its very name, in Chinese, wishes you prosperity for the New Year.

    1 cup thinly sliced lotus roots
    1 cup thinly sliced carrots
    1 cup thinly sliced bamboo shoots
    3 water chestnuts: peel, wash, slice thinly
   12 dried Chinese black mushrooms: soak in hot water
        for 30 minutes, until softened, wash, remove
        stems
   30 pieces of dried tiger lily buds: soak, cut off bottom
        ends
   ¼ cup Chinese celery, cut into julienne strips 1½ inches
        long
   ¾ cup snow peas: remove strings and ends, slice thinly
    4 slices of dried bean curd, soaked and sliced
   ½ cup gingko nuts, peeled and boiled (see page 203)
    1 teaspoon salt
  1½ teaspoons sugar
    1 teaspoon sesame oil
  1½ teaspoons dark soy sauce
    1 tablespoon cornstarch
      Pinch of white pepper
   ¼ cup vegetable broth (see page 49) or cold water
  2½ to 3 tablespoons peanut oil
    1 piece of fresh ginger, 1 inch long, peeled
    1 package (2 ounces) bean thread noodles: soak for 30
        minutes, drain

1.   Prepare all vegetables, bean curd, and gingko nuts. Arrange in piles on a plate. In a small bowl mix ½ teaspoon salt, the sugar, sesame oil, soy sauce, cornstarch, white pepper, and broth or cold water. Set aside.

2.   Heat a wok over high heat for 45 seconds; add peanut oil, ginger, and ½ teaspoon salt. Use a spatula to coat the sides of the wok with oil. Begin adding vegetables. First stir-fry lotus root, then add carrots and remaining vegetables. Stir-fry continuously just until snow peas turn bright green.

3.   As you stir-fry, add about ½ cup water, a little at a time, to create steam for the cooking. Add the soaked, drained bean thread noodles and stir-fry them.

4.   Make a well in the center of the ingredients. Pour in reserved soy-sauce and cornstarch mixture, cover the well with the vegetables, and stir-fry for 2 more minutes. Taste: The ingredients may need a bit more cooking. Vegetables should be crisp-tender and the cornstarch cooked. Remove, place in a serving dish, and serve immediately.

NOTE: Many people prefer this dish served with plain cooked rice.

YOK FAR
BUN
LOP
CHEUNG

*Broccoli and
Lop Cheung*

On New Year's Day to eat *lop cheung* is to partake of a long life. Broccoli is a symbol of jade, itself symbolic of good health and youth.

> 6 pieces of Chinese sausage (*lop cheung*)
>   Flowers from 1 bunch of broccoli, cut off about 1½
>   inches from the top
> 2 tablespoons peanut oil
> 1 slice of fresh ginger
> ½ teaspoon salt
> 1 tablespoon white wine

1. Steam sausage for 20 minutes (see steaming directions, page 46).

2. While sausage is steaming, wash broccoli and drain off excess water. When sausage is thoroughly steamed through, cut it into diagonal slices ⅛ inch thick. Reserve in a preheated serving dish, in a warm oven.

3. Heat a wok over high heat for 45 seconds. Add peanut oil. Add ginger and salt. When a wisp of white smoke appears, add broccoli and stir-fry for 2 minutes. Pour white wine around edge of wok, allowing it to trickle down the sides. This will create some steam, and broccoli will turn bright green. When it turns bright green, it is done.

4. Turn off heat, remove broccoli from wok, and surround the sausages with the flowers. Serve immediately.

SAH
DEH
NGAU
YUK

Beef Saté

This preparation made its way into China from Singapore and Malaysia. The Cantonese are particularly fond of the beef with its strong curry flavor.

½ cup dark soy sauce
2¼ tablespoons curry powder
¼ teaspoon salt
Pinch of white pepper
5½ tablespoons honey
2 pounds flank steak, cut into 1-inch cubes
3 to 4 tablespoons peanut oil

1. Mix 2½ tablespoons dark soy sauce with the curry powder. Mix well together; set aside.

2. Place salt, white pepper, and honey in a large bowl. Add ¼ cup dark soy sauce, stir together, then add curry mixture. Add the remainder of the dark soy sauce and mix well.

3. Place cubes of beef in the curry mixture. Allow beef to stand for at least 8 hours, preferably overnight, refrigerated.

4. Place peanut oil in the bottom of a shallow frying pan, to cover the bottom. Brown beef cubes for 1 minute on each side, until they become light brown in color. Remove to a baking pan, placing cubes in a single layer. Add frying pan juices. The overnight marinade may be added as well to make more sauce.

5. Place the baking pan in a preheated broiler and broil for 3 to 7 minutes, according to meat preference—rare, medium, or well done. Serve immediately.

NOTE: Beef saté can be prepared ahead completely; reheat in the oven. It can be frozen; before reheating, allow to defrost and come to room temperature.

YUE
CHI
TONG

*Shark's-Fin
Soup*

No banquet as important as that on New Year's Day would be considered complete without shark's-fin soup. In Canton and Hong Kong, where such soups are rated by the quality and rarity of as many as 20 different species of shark, the soup can be as expensive as an entire banquet. To prepare it in the traditional manner requires some time, but the result is worth the effort.

    2 ounces dry shark's fin
    2 cups cold water
    1 tablespoon white vinegar
    1 tablespoon white wine
    2 scallions: wash, dry, discard both ends, cut into
       halves
    1 large slice of ginger
    1 piece of pork fat, 2 inches square, cut into 3 pieces
    1 cup chicken broth (see page 48), to steam shark's fin
    3 cups cold water
    8 ounces chicken cutlet
5½ cups chicken broth
 ¾ cup bamboo shoots, shredded
    1 cup snow peas, shredded
3½ tablespoons cornstarch mixed with 3½ tablespoons
       cold water
    1 teaspoon sesame oil

1.   Soak the shark's fin until it becomes soft, then wash and rinse in a fine strainer. Soak overnight in a bowl with 2 cups cold water and the white vinegar. Drain, then place in a dish with wine, scallions, ginger, and pork fat. Steam with the chicken broth for 30 minutes (see steaming directions, page 46). Discard all ingredients except shark's fin. Wash, drain through a fine strainer, and set aside. There should be ½ cup shark's fin.

2.   Bring 3 cups cold water to a boil in a pot and cook the chicken cutlet for 4 to 5 minutes. Remove pot from heat, run cold water into pot, and drain chicken. Remove chicken from pot, allow to cool, cut into julienne, and set aside.

3.   Pour the chicken broth into a pot. Add shark's fin, cover, and bring to a boil. Lower heat and simmer for 20 minutes.

4.   Add sliced chicken and bamboo shoots and bring to a boil. Add snow peas and again bring to a boil. Add cornstarch mixture slowly, stirring constantly until soup thickens. Turn off heat, add sesame oil, and blend in. Pour into a preheated tureen and serve.

NOTE: If you compare the amount of soup in this recipe with other soups in this book, you will find that it is less. This is deliberate. Shark's-fin soup is a most elegant, very special banquet preparation and generally only a small bowl is served as a course. It is a tradition of which I approve.

脆皮糯米鸡

CHOI PEI
NOR MAI
GAI

*Kwangtung
Crispy Stuffed
Chicken*

This is most definitely a New Year recipe. It takes some time to prepare, but to serve it is immediately perceived as a gesture of great respect by those who receive it. It is a difficult recipe, but it is so delicious that it is worth *any* effort. It is so special that it cannot be ordered in restaurants, even in the finest in China, on short notice. It must be reserved well in advance of your feast.

1 fresh whole chicken, 3 to 3½ pounds

For marinade for the chicken, combine in a bowl and mix well:
  ½ teaspoon ginger juice mixed with 1½ teaspoons white wine
  ½ teaspoon salt
  2 teaspoons sugar
  1½ tablespoons oyster sauce
  1½ teaspoons sesame oil
  1½ teaspoons light soy sauce
  2 tablespoons cornstarch
     Pinch of white pepper

½ pound raw shrimp: shell, devein, wash, dry, dice

For marinade for shrimp, combine in a bowl and mix well:
  ½ teaspoon ginger juice mixed with 1 teaspoon white wine
  ¼ teaspoon salt
  ½ teaspoon sugar
  1 teaspoon oyster sauce
  ½ teaspoon sesame oil
  ½ teaspoon light soy sauce
  1 teaspoon cornstarch
     Pinch of white pepper

1 cup fresh pork, cut into ¼-inch cubes

For marinade for pork, combine in a bowl and mix well:
- ½ teaspoon ginger juice mixed with 1 teaspoon white wine
- ¼ teaspoon salt
- ¾ teaspoon sugar
- 1 teaspoon oyster sauce
- ¾ teaspoon sesame oil
- ½ teaspoon light soy sauce
- 1½ teaspoons cornstarch
- Pinch of white pepper

- 5½ tablespoons peanut oil, for stir-frying
- 3 garlic cloves, minced
- 1 slice of fresh ginger
- 6 dried Chinese black mushrooms: soak in hot water for 30 minutes, wash, discard stems, cut into ⅛-inch dice
- 1¾ cups glutinous rice
- 1¾ cups cold water
- 6 fresh water chestnuts: peel, wash, dry, cut into ⅛-inch dice
- 6 scallions: wash, dry, discard both ends, slice finely
- 5 cups peanut oil, for deep-frying

1. Bone the chicken: Follow instructions for boning as set down for boning duck in Eight-Jewel Duck recipe (page 169). The only difference is that with the chicken the thigh meat and bone and half of the drumstick meat and bone are removed, whereas with the duck they are left intact. Cut chicken meat into ½-inch dice.

2. Marinate chicken, shrimp, and pork for 30 minutes each.

3. Place a wok over high heat. Add 2 tablespoons peanut oil and coat the wok with a spatula. Add 1 minced garlic clove. When it browns, add boned chicken meat and stir-fry for 3 minutes, until chicken turns white. Remove; set aside. Wash wok.

4. Place wok again over high heat, pour in 2 tablespoons peanut oil, and coat the wok. Add the slice of ginger and 1 minced garlic clove. When garlic browns, add shrimp and stir-fry for 2 minutes, or until they turn pink. Remove and set aside. Wash the wok.

5. Place wok again over high heat. Pour in 1½ tablespoons peanut oil, coat the wok, and add 1 minced garlic clove. When garlic browns, add mushrooms and stir-fry for 10 seconds. Add diced pork and stir-fry for 3 minutes, or until it whitens. Remove and set aside. Wash the wok.

6. Cook the rice: Follow precisely the procedure for steaming glutinous rice, as set down in the recipe for Eight-Jewel Duck (see page 171). When rice is cooked, place it in a large bowl and allow to cool.

7. Place reserved chicken, shrimp, and pork as well as water chestnuts and scallions on top of rice in bowl. Combine all ingredients with your hands, thoroughly.

8. With a large needle and heavy-duty thread, sew up neck cavity of boned chicken. Stuff the chicken with the contents of the bowl. Sew up rear opening. Pat the chicken into the shape of a normal bird.

9. Preheat the oven to 300° to 325° F. and roast the chicken on a rack in a roasting pan for 1½ to 2 hours. Midway through the process turn the chicken over. Roast until it is brown, then remove from oven. Allow to cool, for 4 to 5 hours.

10. Place a wok over high heat, add 5 cups peanut oil, and heat to the boiling point. When white smoke appears, place chicken in a large Chinese strainer and lower into boiling oil. Deep-fry until skin becomes golden brown and crisp, 7 to 10 minutes. If the entire chicken cannot be submerged in oil then ladle the boiling oil over it until it becomes crisp.

11. Remove chicken from wok and allow it to drain for at least 2 minutes. Place chicken on a platter, slice, and serve immediately.

NOTE: The chicken can be boned a day earlier, if desired. After it is roasted and allowed to cool, it can be frozen. To complete cooking, allow to defrost, place in a 350° F. oven for 30 minutes, then deep-fry.

豉蒜豬肫	SEE SIU JUE BEI
	Soy Sauce Roast Ham

In China this dish is traditionally prepared by cooking a pork shoulder, with fat and skin intact, atop the stove with honey and soy sauce. It is quite greasy. My version eliminates virtually all of the fat and the ham is most tender.

8½ pounds fresh ham, shank half: have butcher remove
　　　the skin, but leave a thin layer of fat
　6 garlic cloves, peeled, cut into ¼-inch slices
　½ teaspoon salt
　¾ cup dark soy sauce
　4 teaspoons sugar
　¼ teaspoon white pepper
　4 cups cold water

1. Preheat oven to 375° F. for 15 minutes.

2. Place ham in a roasting pan. Use a knife to cut slits in sides of ham, and insert slices of garlic into slits. Mix salt, soy sauce, sugar, and white pepper and use mixture to coat ham thoroughly. Pour ¾ cup cold water into the roasting pan and put ham in oven.

3. Roast ham at 375° F. for 30 minutes. Reduce heat to 350° F. for 1½ hours. After 1 hour place foil on both ends of ham to prevent drying out. Reduce heat to 325° F. for 2 hours; turn ham over. Reduce heat to 300° F. for 1 hour; turn ham once again. Reduce heat to 275° F. for 2 hours, then to 250° F. for the final 2 hours. Baste every 30 minutes, adding a little water after each basting.

After 5½ hours insert a chopstick into the ham. If it goes in easily the ham is done. This is possible because a young ham can be extra tender. The ham should be tested every 30 minutes.

When ham is cooked, remove, carve, and serve immediately on a platter with the liquid (2 cups) which remains in the pan.

NOTE: The ham can be prepared 4 to 5 days in advance and kept refrigerated. It can be frozen for 4 to 5 weeks. Before reheating in the oven, allow it to defrost and to come to room temperature. When reheating, place the liquid residue in the pan.

揚	YANGZHOU
州	CHAU
炒	FAN
飯	*Fried Rice Yangzhou Style*

Fried rice is perhaps everybody's favorite Chinese dish. Certainly it is the most familiar. It can be prepared in many ways, but for the Chinese the highest form of preparation is in the style of Yangzhou, considered the best in the country. Traditionally the frying done is with lard (pork fat), so that is the way it is set down here. Peanut oil may be used, in identical amounts.

4 ounces shrimp: shell, devein, wash, dry, cut into ¼-inch pieces

To make a marinade for shrimp, combine in a bowl and mix well:
   ¼ teaspoon salt
   ¼ teaspoon sugar
   ½ teaspoon light soy sauce
   ¾ teaspoon oyster sauce
   ½ teaspoon sesame oil
   ½ teaspoon white wine
   ½ teaspoon ginger juice
      Pinch of white pepper

3 eggs, beaten with pinch of white pepper and ⅛
    teaspoon salt
5½ tablespoons lard or peanut oil
  1 cup diced roast pork (see page 70)
  2 garlic cloves, minced
  1 slice of fresh ginger
1½ cups cooked rice (see recipe for cooking rice, page
    47), cooked in advance, even a day earlier, then
    cooled to room temperature
  ¼ teaspoon salt
  1 tablespoon light soy sauce
  3 scallions: discard both ends, wash, dry, slice finely

1. Marinate shrimp for 30 minutes.

2. Stir-fry separately, and reserve, in this order, the following ingredients. Wash wok and spatula after first 3 fryings.

Beaten eggs in 1½ tablespoons of lard, until soft but not dry.

Roast pork with 1 minced garlic clove in 1 tablespoon lard.

Marinated shrimp mixture with 1 minced garlic clove, and the slice of fresh ginger, in 1 tablespoon lard.

Rice with ¼ teaspoon salt in 2 tablespoons lard. Before stir-frying rice, loosen grains with chopsticks or hands so there are no lumps.

3. When rice is hot, add pork and mix thoroughly. Add shrimp and mix thoroughly. Add soy sauce, stir in, then add scrambled eggs, which have been broken into small pieces. Add scallions and mix all ingredients very thoroughly. Place on a serving platter and serve immediately.

NOTE: For those who prefer a darker fried rice, substitute 1 tablespoon dark soy sauce for the light sauce called for in the recipe.

This can be prepared in advance, but only to the point just before the scallions are added. They must be put in freshly. Fried rice may also be frozen for a brief time, for no more than 2 weeks, and reheated.

脆皮西班	CHOY PEI SEK BON
	Crispy *Sea Bass*

A fish must always be served in the latter part of a New Year's banquet, because a fish, any fish, symbolizes reproductive powers and therefore is at this particular time of the year representative of regeneration. It is the New Year itself!

1 whole sea bass, 2 pounds

To make a marinade for the fish, combine:
1½ tablespoons white wine
  1 teaspoon salt
  1 teaspoon white vinegar
    Pinch of white pepper

  6 cups peanut oil
  1 egg, beaten
  ¾ cup cornstarch
  ½ cup onions, cut into ¼-inch dice
2½ tablespoons shallots, cut into ⅛-inch dice
  1 teaspoon minced ginger
  1 teaspoon minced garlic

To make a sauce, combine in a bowl and mix well:
  1 tablespoon white vinegar
1½ teaspoons sugar
  ¼ teaspoon salt
4½ tablespoons catsup
  1 teaspoon dark soy sauce
2½ teaspoons Hunan pepper (see hot oil, page 20)
  ½ teaspoon preserved horse beans
    Pinch of white pepper
  1 teaspoon Shao-Hsing wine or sherry
  1 tablespoon cornstarch
  5 ounces chicken broth

  2 scallions, finely sliced
  2 sprigs of coriander

1.   Wash fish, remove membranes, dry with paper towels. Make 4 cuts on each side of the body. Place fish on a large dish. Pour on marinade and use hands to rub it in, coating the fish evenly. Let it sit for 15 minutes.

2.   Heat a wok over high heat for 1 minute; add peanut oil. As oil heats, coat fish with beaten egg, including the cuts in the skin. Spread cornstarch on a sheet of wax paper and place fish on it. Coat body thoroughly with cornstarch, including the cuts in the skin. Shake off excess cornstarch.

3.   By this time the oil should be heated and a wisp of white smoke should appear. Place fish in a Chinese strainer and lower it into the oil. Deep-fry for 10 minutes, until fish browns. Tip the fish's tail and head into the oil if the fish is too large, to ensure that it will be fully cooked. If needed, you may use a ladle to pour hot oil over these parts. When fish is browned, remove from oil and allow to drain over a bowl.

4.   Pour oil from wok. Wipe off with paper towel. Replace 2 tablespoons oil in the wok. Stir-fry onions and shallots in the oil for 4 to 5 minutes, until they brown. Add ginger and garlic; stir together for 45 seconds. Stir the sauce and pour into the wok. Mix all ingredients thoroughly, until sauce thickens and bubbles.

5.   Place fish on a preheated platter, pour sauce over it, sprinkle with sliced scallions, and serve immediately with a coriander garnish.

A B A N Q U E T   O F   S W E E T S

JAU LONG *Sweet Wine Rice*

JAU LONG TONG *Sweet Wine Rice Soup*

DON PING GUA *Steamed Apples*

BUT SEE HEUNG JIU *Honey-Glazed Bananas*

JAR SEUT GOH *Fried Ice Cream*

SWEETS

The Last Course

The Chinese do not eat sweet desserts, as Westerners do, at the end of their meals. They prefer fresh fruit such as apples, especially the hard, green, somewhat tart apples that are found throughout the country. They also frequently eat oranges, tangerines, pears, and grapes. In subtropical Canton they also enjoy fresh pineapple, papaya, mangos, and various melons. Such sweets as pastries and water chestnut cakes are never served as desserts; they are for the dim sum teahouse. Occasionally the Chinese will eat a sweet soup as a dinner course, perhaps a soup made from lotus seeds or gingko nuts.

However, most Westerners prefer to have a sweet as a final course. You may wish to conclude your banquet with Honey Walnuts (see page 73), or you may wish to try any of the following. These are traditional Chinese sweets, with ice cream a *new* tradition, of Canton and Hong Kong, imported from the West.

JAU
LONG

*Sweet Wine
Rice*

This is a well-known food preparation in Shanghai, where it is eaten as a snack and also used to prepare Shanghai's equally famous sweet Wine Rice Soup. The sweetness of the rice is due to its fermentation. Only when a soup is made is more sweetness added, in the form of sugar.

2 cups glutinous rice
2 cups cold water
4 or 5 cups water, for steaming
1 wine pill, crushed
1 teaspoon flour

1.   Wash rice 2 or 3 times; drain off excess water thoroughly. Place rice in an 8-inch cake pan, add 2 cups cold water, and place the cake pan in a steamer. Add 4 to 5 cups water to a wok, bring to a boil, and steam rice for 30 to 40 minutes, or until it is cooked (see steaming directions, page 46).

2.   Place cooked rice in a large mixing bowl, run cold water into it, and loosen rice with your fingers. Drain off water. Place the crushed wine pill in the rice and mix it into the rice with your hands, thoroughly. When mixed, use your fingers to punch 8 to 10 holes into the rice (this aids the fermentation process).

3.   Sprinkle the flour on top of the rice, cover the bowl with a damp cloth, and set it in an unheated gas oven, or in a warm place. The rice will ferment in 24 to 48 hours. You know fermentation has occurred when you see bubbles and liquid in the holes you made in the rice.

NOTE: Sweet Wine Rice may be stored in a tightly closed jar, refrigerated. It will keep for 2 to 3 months. It is also available in jars in Chinatown or Asian food stores. Once opened, it must be refrigerated.

| 酒釀湯 | JAU LONG TONG |
| | *Sweet Wine Rice Soup* |

1 cup glutinous rice powder
½ cup warm water
10 eggs
5 cups water
1½ cups wine rice (see page 230)
½ cup sugar

1. Make glutinous rice balls: Mix 1 cup glutinous rice powder with ½ cup warm water by placing powder on a work surface, making a well in the center, and slowly adding the water, mixing with the fingers as you do so until water is absorbed. Knead into a dough. Make 40 rice balls, slightly larger than marble-size, about ½ inch in diameter. Set aside.

2. Break each egg and slide it, without breaking the yolk, into an individual bowl.

3. Pour the water into a wok and bring to a boil. Add wine rice and sugar and heat through for 1 to 2 minutes. Add the eggs, one by one, and continue cooking until they are somewhat poached. The eggs should be cooked but the yolks not hardened. Add the glutinous rice balls and cook for 2 to 3 minutes, until balls change color and float to the top.

4. Serve wine rice soup in rice bowls, making sure each bowl contains a measure of soup and wine rice, 1 egg, and 4 rice balls.

DON
PING
GUA

*Steamed
Apples*

This is another sweet created by those inventive chefs in Shanghai. What makes this so special is the "soup" that is created by the condensation as the apples steam. It is naturally sweet and refreshing.

 8 cups cold water
 4 tablespoons white vinegar
10 small- to medium-size apples
 1 cup sweet red bean paste

1. Put water and vinegar in a large mixing bowl. Keep at hand.

2. Cut tops off apples, about one quarter of the way down. Reserve tops. Place apples immediately in vinegar-water to keep from browning. Scoop out cores of apples and a bit of the sides, and fill the holes with 1 to 2 teaspoons red bean paste.

3. Place each apple in a small Chinese rice bowl or soup bowl, arrange in a steamer, place tops of apples back on, and steam for 30 minutes (see steaming directions, page 46).

4. The apples are done when they are slightly soft to the touch and when there is a bit of condensed juice in the bowls. The apples should be served immediately, hot. They are rich, sweet, tart, tasty.

NOTE: Other fillings such as lotus-seed paste, black bean paste, chestnut purée, or date filling can be substituted for the red bean paste, but the last is the traditional filling.

BUT
SEE
HEUNG
JIU

*Honey-Glazed
Bananas*

This popular sweet originated in either Canton or Shang-hai, nobody seems to know which. It doesn't make any difference where, because it is made beautifully in both places.

To make batter, combine:
1 cup flour
2 teaspoons baking powder
7 ounces water, at room temperature
1 tablespoon peanut oil

2 large or 3 medium-size firm bananas
4 to 5 cups peanut oil

To make glaze, combine:
¾ cup water
¾ cup sugar

Bowl of ice water

1. Make batter by mixing ingredients in a bowl. If too dry, add a little more water. The batter should resemble pancake batter.

2. Break the bananas into 10 equal pieces, each about 1½ inches long. Drop banana pieces into the batter and coat evenly.

3. Heat a wok over high heat for 1 minute. Add peanut oil and heat until a wisp of white smoke appears. Deep-fry the batter-coated bananas for 3 to 4 minutes, until pieces turn golden brown and crunchy. Remove from oil, drain, and set aside.

4. Empty oil from the wok into a bowl. Wash wok thoroughly until it is totally free of oil.

Deep-fat fry for 3 to 4 minutes

5. Make the glaze: Add ¾ cup water to the wok and bring to a boil. Add the sugar and stir until sugar is dissolved and glaze is bubbling. Allow glaze to boil until it begins to reduce and thicken, 5 to 6 minutes. The sugar glaze is ready when a drop solidifies when dropped into cold water.

6. Place bananas in the glaze and stir until well coated. Dip each coated banana into ice water. The glaze will harden instantly into a candylike finish. Serve immediately.

NOTE: Frying bananas with glaze is traditional; however, they can be prepared without the final glaze. Simply add a tablespoon of sugar to the batter and serve after you have fried the bananas.

炸雪糕 JAR SEUT GOH

Fried Ice Cream

People are often startled to hear that there is ice cream in China, but in fact ice cream, a Western import, has been part of the menus of Canton, Hong Kong, and Shanghai for some time. If you'd like a treat, stop in at the Tah Dah Restaurant on Nanking Road in Shanghai and try one of their ice cream sodas.

 6 cups peanut oil
 1 package (about 10 ounces) sliced raw almonds
10 scoops of vanilla ice cream

1.   Heat a wok over high heat; pour in 4 cups peanut oil. When a wisp of white smoke appears, place almonds in a strainer and lower into the oil. Fry for 10 seconds, remove from oil, allow to drain and cool. Strain oil and reserve.

Roll each scoop of ice cream in the almonds until well coated.

2.   Spread almonds on a platter. Roll each scoop of ice cream around in the almonds until it is well coated. Mold the ice cream ball with your hands, pressing the nuts into it gently. Repeat. After each two, place them in the freezer. Repeat until 10 almond-covered balls have been made. Freeze for at least 24 hours, until rock hard.

3.   Heat the wok over high heat and add the reserved oil plus 2 additional cups. When the wisp of smoke appears, the oil is ready. Place each ice cream ball in a strainer and lower into the oil for 8 to 10 seconds. Remove, place in a dessert bowl that has been kept in the freezer, and serve immediately.

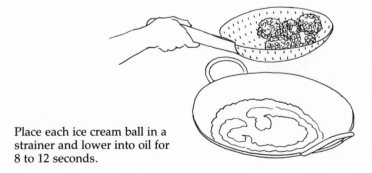

Place each ice cream ball in a strainer and lower into oil for 8 to 12 seconds.

| 好食後語 | # HO HO SIK |
| | ## A Few Last Words |

My father used to tell me that a fine meal, well cooked and in ample, satisfying portions, was a blessing from the gods; that good food and the ability to enjoy it was more important than wealth. "Money," he would say, "cannot buy a good stomach."

When you cook, don't skimp, either on food or on a good brandy to go with it, he would say. I agree with that and it is my wish that as you go about creating Chinese banquets from this book, you pay attention to my father. Ho Ho Sik. Good Eating.

Eileen Yin-Fei Lo

Index

almonds, in fried ice cream, 235
apples, steamed, 232

bacon, fresh, preserved vegetables with, 166
bamboo chopsticks, 38–39
bamboo steamer, 38
bananas, honey-glazed, 233–234
bass, *see* sea bass; striped bass
batter-fried oysters, 182–183
bean curd, 14–15
   panfried with scallions, 204
   Shanghai fish rolled in, 128
   stuffed, Hakka-style, 161–162
beans, four-season, 141–142
bean sprout salad, Shanghai, 125
beef, 31
   five-spice, 71
   orange, 148–149
   pepper steak, 80–81
   and pickled Shanghai cabbage, 118–119
   saté, with flank steak, 217
   and sour mustard pickle, 172–173
   Szechuan, 136–137
   twice-fried shredded, 95–96

beer, 34, 36
black beans, 15
   clams with, 213–214
   shrimp with, 187–188
blanching, 45–46
bok choy with oyster sauce, Shanghai, 184
boning fowl, 52
brandy, 34, 36
broccoli and lop cheung, 216
broths, 48–49
brown bean sauce, marinated shrimp in, 65–66
Buddha's delight, 214–215

cabbage, peppery, 145
cabbage, Shanghai, 16
   pickled, beef and, 118–119
cabbage, Tientsin, 16–17
   spicy, 64–65
   stir-fried, 109
Canton banquet, 74–91
   lemon chicken, 84–85
   pepper steak, 80–81
   shrimp with lobster sauce, 78–79

silk squash soup with shredded pork, 82–83

Singapore noodles, 88–89

steamed duck with preserved plums, 81–82

steamed sea bass, 90–91

sweet and sour pork, 86–87

water dumplings with chives, 77–78

carp, 32

carrot flowerets, 58

cauliflower ferns, 57

chicken, 29–30

beggar's, 105–107

boiled, Ching Ping market style, 66–67

broth (stock), 48

dragon soup, 122–123

hacked, 68–69

with hoisin sauce, 116–117

Hunan pepper, 147

Kwangtung crispy stuffed, 220–223

lemon, 84–85

perfumed, 139

salt-baked, 164–165

Singapore noodles, 88–89

velvet wintermelon soup, 137–138

chives:

and crab meat with noodles, pan-fried, 190–191

water dumplings with, 77–78

choi sum, stir-fried, 201

Choy banquet (food from the earth), 194–209

bean curd panfried with scallions, 204

spicy rice noodles, 200–201

steamed whole wintermelon soup, 202–203

stir-fried choi sum, 201

vegetarian fish, 208–209

vegetarian goose, 198–199

vegetarian oysters, 197–198

vegetarian stuffed lotus leaves, 206–207

vegetarian sweet and sour pork, 205–206

chopsticks:

bamboo, 38–39

eating with, 60

clams with black beans, 213–214

cleavers:

Chinese, 38

working with, 50–51

Cognac, 34, 36

cold sesame noodles, 132

crab meat and chives with noodles, pan-fried, 190–191

cucumbers, in vegetable sculpture, 54–57

curry powder, 17

deep-frying, 44–45

Dim Sum Book, The: Classic Recipes from the Chinese Teahouse (Yin-Fei Lo), 35

dragon soup, 122–123

Dragon Well tea, 36

drinks, for Chinese banquets, 34–36

duck, 30

eight-jewel stuffed, 168–171

Peking, 96–99

steamed, with preserved plums, 81–82

tea-smoked, 124–125

dumplings, water, with chives, 77–78

earth, food from the, *see* Choy banquet

eastern cooking, *see* Shanghai banquet

eggplant with garlic sauce, 155–156

eggplants, Chinese, vegetarian oysters, 197–198

equipment, in Chinese cooking, 37–39

first course, 62–73
  boiled chicken, Ching Ping market style, 66–67
  five-spice beef, 71
  ginger pickle, 72
  hacked chicken, 68–69
  honey walnuts, 73
  marinated shrimp in brown bean sauce, 65–66
  roast pork, 70
  spicy Tientsin cabbage, 64–65
  steamed black mushrooms, 64
fish:
  broth (stock), 49
  rolled in bean curd, Shanghai, 128
  shopping guide to, 31–33
  Szechuan panfried, 142–143
  see also sea bass; *specific fish*
fish, vegetarian, 208–209

flounder, 32

foods, for Chinese banquets, 13–33

fowl:
  boning and cutting, 52
  shopping guide to, 29–30

garlic sauce:
  eggplant with, 155–156
  shredded pork with, 152–153
ginger, 18
  pickled, 19, 72
  soup, 150–151
goose, vegetarian, 198–199

green tea, 19, 36

Gung Hay Fat Choy banquet (cooking for a Happy New Year), 210–227
  beef saté, 217
  broccoli and lop cheung, 216
  Buddha's delight, 214–215
  clams with black beans, 213–214
  crispy sea bass, 226–227
  fried fice Yangzhou style, 224–225
  Kwangtung crispy stuffed chicken, 220–223
  shark's-fin soup, 218–219
  soy sauce roast ham, 223–224

Hakka banquet (cooking of the nomads), 158–177
  beef and sour mustard pickle, 172–173
  black and white mushrooms, 174–175
  eight-jewel stuffed duck, 168–171
  preserved vegetables with fresh bacon, 166
  salt-baked chicken, 164–165
  -style, lotus leaf rice, 175–177
  -style, stuffed bean curd, 161–162
  watercress soup with meatballs, 167
  white water shrimp, 163
ham:
  roast, soy sauce and, 223–224
  see also pork
Hoi Sin banquet (food from the water), 178–193
  batter-fried oysters, 182–183
  panfried noodles with crab meat and chives, 190–191
  seafood wintermelon soup, 186–187
  Shanghai bok choy with oyster sauce, 184
  shrimp with black beans, 187–188

steamed lobster, 185
stuffed scallops, 181–182
Szechuan peppercorn salt, 183
three seas, 188–189
white water fish, 192–193
hoisin sauce, 20
chicken with, 116–117
hot and sour soup, 104–105
Hunan banquet, 144–157
eggplant with garlic sauce, 155–156
ginger soup, 150–151
hot and crisp fish, 156–157
orange beef, 148–149
pepper chicken, 147
peppery cabbage, 145
shredded pork with garlic sauce, 152–153
spicy shrimp, 146
stir-fried leeks with lamb, 154–155

ice cream, fried, 235
ingredients for Chinese banquets, 13–33
introduction to Chinese banquets, 1–9

Jasmine tea, 36

Kwangtung crispy stuffed chicken, 220–223

lamb:
with leeks, stir-fried, 154–155
sliced, with scallions, 102–103
last course, 228–235
fried ice cream, 235
honey-glazed bananas, 233–234
steamed apples, 232
sweet wine rice, 230
sweet wine rice soup, 231

leeks with lamb, stir-fried, 154–155
lemon chicken, 84–85
Lichee Black tea, 36
lobster, 33
dragon soup, 122–123
panfried, 101–102
spicy, 134–135
steamed, 185
three seas, 188–189
Long Jin tea, 36
lop cheung, 20
broccoli and, 216
lotus leaves, 21
rice, Hakka-style, 175–177
vegetarian stuffed, 206–207
Lung Ching tea, 36

meat, shopping guide to, 31
meatballs, watercress soup with, 167
Mou-Tai, 36
mushrooms, Chinese black, 21–22
Buddha's delight, 214–215
steamed, 64
vegetarian goose, 198–199
and white, 174–175

New Year, cooking for a Happy, see Gung Hay Fat Choy banquet
nomad cooking, see Hakka banquet
noodles, egg:
cold sesame, 132
with crab meat and chives, panfried, 190–191
panfried, 126–127
noodles, rice, 23
Singapore, 88–89
spicy, 200–201
northern cooking, see Peking banquet

oil-blanching, 45
oil, scallion, 24
oolong tea, 36
orange beef, 148–149
oysters, batter-fried, 182–183
oysters, vegetarian, 197–198
oyster sauce, 23
   Shanghai bok choy with, 184

pancakes, 99–100
   moo shoo pork, 107–108
Peking banquet, 92–111
   beggar's chicken, 105–107
   duck, 96–99
   hot and sour soup, 104–105
   moo shoo pork, 107–108
   mythical fish, 110–111
   pancakes, 99–100
   panfried lobster, 101–102
   sliced lamb with scallions, 102–103
   stir-fried Tientsin cabbage, 109
   twice-fried shredded beef, 95–96
pepper, green, steak, 80–81
pepper, red, and cabbage, 145
peppercorn salt, Szechuan, 183
peppers, hot, and cabbage, 145
pickle, sour mustard, beef and, 172–173
pickled ginger, 19, 72
plums, preserved, steamed duck with, 81–82
pork, 31
   four-season beans, 141–142
   ginger soup, 150–151
   hot and sour soup, 104–105
   Kwangtung crispy stuffed chicken, 220–223
   moo shoo, 107–108
   panfried lobster, 101–102
   panfried noodles, 126–127

roast, 70
   shredded with garlic sauce, 152–153
   shredded, silk squash soup with, 82–83
   shrimp with lobster sauce, 78–79
   spider shrimp, 132–134
   stew, 120–121
   sweet and sour, 86–87
   Szechuan panfried fish, 142–143
   vegetarian sweet and sour, 205–206
   water dumplings with chives, 77–78
   white cut, 140–141
poultry, *see* fowl; *specific poultry*

red bean paste, 23
red snapper, 32
rice:
   cooking, 47–48
   fried, Yangzhou style, 224–225
   lotus leaf, Hakka-style, 175–177
   sweet wine, 230
   vegetarian stuffed lotus leaves, 206–207
rice noodles, *see* noodles, rice

salad, Shanghai bean-sprout, 125
salt, Szechuan peppercorn, 183
salt-baked chicken, 164–165
saté, beef, 217
sauces:
   brown bean, 65–66
   garlic, 152–153, 155–156
   hoisin sauce, 116–117
   for lobster, shrimp with, 78–79
   oyster, 184
   salt-baked chicken, 165
   white cut pork, 140–141
   see also specific banquet recipes

sausage, Chinese:
    broccoli and, 216
    see also lop cheung
scallion oil, 24
scallions:
    flowers, 58
    panfried with bean curd, 204
    sliced lamb with, 102–103
scallops, 33
    stuffed, 181–182
sculpture, vegetable, 53–59
sea bass, 32
    crispy, 226–227
    hot and crisp, 156–157
    mythical, 110–111
    steamed, 90–91
    white water, 192–193
seafood, 31–33, 178, 193
    shopping guide to, 31–33
    wintermelon soup, 186–187
    see also specific seafood
sesame noodles, cold, 132
Shanghai banquet, 112–128
    bean-sprout salad, 125
    beef and pickled Shanghai cabbage,
        118–119
    chicken with hoisin sauce, 116–117
    crystal shrimp, 115–116
    dragon soup, 122–123
    fish rolled in bean curd, 128
    panfried noodles, 126–127
    pork stew, 120–121
    tea-smoked duck, 124–125
Shao-Hsing wine, 25, 36
shark's-fin soup, 218–219
shrimp, 32
    with black beans, 187–188
    crystal, 115–116

eight-jewel stuffed duck, 168–171
fried rice Yangzhou style, 224–225
Hunan spicy, 146
Kwangtung crispy stuffed chicken,
    220–223
with lobster sauce, 78–79
lotus leaf rice, Hakka-style, 175–177
marinated, in brown bean sauce, 65–
    66
seafood wintermelon soup, 186–187
spider, 132–134
stuffed bean curd, Hakka-style, 161–
    162
stuffed scallops, 181–182
three seas, 188–189
water dumplings with chives, 77–78
white water, 163
Soi Sin tea, 36
soups:
    dragon, 122–123
    ginger, 150–151
    hot and sour, 104–105
    seafood wintermelon, 186–187
    shark's-fin, 218–219
    silk squash, with shredded pork, 82–
        83
    steamed whole wintermelon, 202–203
    sweet wine rice, 231
    velvet wintermelon, 137–138
    watercress, with meatballs, 167
soup spoon, Chinese, eating with, 60
sour mustard pickle and beef, 172–173
southern cooking, *see* Canton banquet
soy sauce, 26
    roast ham, 223–224
spatula, Chinese, 38
squash soup, silk, with shredded pork,
    82–83

steak, *see* beef
steamer, bamboo, 38
steaming, 46–47
   preparing porcelain and Pyrex for, 47
stew, pork, 120–121
stir-fried choi sum, 201
stir-fried leeks with lamb, 154–155
stir-fried Tientsin cabbage, 109
stir-frying, 43–44
stocks, 48–49
strainer, Chinese, 39
striped bass, 31
   Szechuan panfried fish, 142–143
sweet and sour pork, 86–87
sweets, *see* last course
Szechuan banquet, 129–143
   beef, 136–137
   cold sesame noodles, 132
   four-season beans, 141–142
   panfried fish, 142–143
   perfumed chicken, 139
   spicy lobster, 134–135
   spider shrimp, 132–134
   velvet wintermelon soup, 137–138
   white cut pork, 140–141

taro root, 27
   vegetarian fish, 208–209
teas, 34
   types of, 36
tea-smoked duck, 124–125
techniques, in Chinese cooking, 40–60
   art of vegetable sculpture, 53–59
   boning fowl, 52
   cooking rice, 47–48
   cooking with the wok, 41–43
   cutting up fowl, 52
   deep-frying, 44–45

eating the Chinese way, 60
oil-blanching, 45–46
preparing broths (stocks), 48–49
preparing porcelain and Pyrex for
   steaming, 47
steaming, 46–47
stir-frying, 43–44
water-blanching, 45–46
working with the cleaver, 50–51
three seas, 188–189
tiger lily buds, 27
   Buddha's delight, 214–215
   hot and sour soup, 104–105
   moo shoo pork, 107–108
Tiht Koon Yum tea, 36
tools, in Chinese cooking, 37–39
turnips:
   basket, 59
   flowers, 57

vegetables:
   broth (stock), 49
   preserved, with fresh bacon, 166
vegetable sculpture, art of, 53–59
   carrot flowerets, 58
   cauliflower ferns, 57
   crab, 55–56
   ferns, 57
   lobster, 54–55
   scallion flowers, 58
   turnip basket, 59
   turnip flowers, 57
vegetarian dishes, 194–209
   broth (stock), 49
   fish, 208–209
   goose, 198–199
   oysters, 197–198

stuffed lotus leaves, 206–207
sweet and sour pork, 205–206

walnuts:
    honey, 73
    vegetarian sweet and sour pork, 205–206
water, food from the, *see* Hoi Sin banquet
water-blanching, 45–46
watercress:
    soup with meatballs, 167
    spider shrimp, 132–134
western cooking, *see* Hunan banquet; Szechuan banquet
whiskey, 34

white cut pork sauce, 140–141
wine rice, sweet, 230
    soup, 231
wines, 34–36
    banquets with, 35
    Chablis, 28–29
    Shao-Hsing, 36
    sweet plum (Mou-Tai), 36
wintermelon, 29
wintermelon soup:
    seafood, 186–187
    steamed whole, 202–203
    velvet, 137–138
wok, 37
    cooking with, 41–43
    ring, 37